FAITH DYNAMICS

KEN CHANT

FAITH DYNAMICS
KEN CHANT

Copyright © 2012 KEN CHANT

ISBN 978-161529-064-2

For information on reordering contact:

Vision Publishing

1672 Main St. E 109

Ramona, CA 92065

1-800-9-VISION

www.booksbyvision.com

All rights reserved worldwide

No part of the book may be reproduced in any manner whatsoever without written permission of the author except in brief quotations embodied in critical articles of reviews.

A NOTE ON GENDER

It is unfortunate that the English language does not contain an adequate generic pronoun (especially in the singular number) that includes without bias both male and female. So *"he, him, his, man, mankind,"* with their plurals, must do the work for both sexes. Accordingly, wherever it is appropriate to do so in the following pages, please include the feminine gender in the masculine, and vice versa.

FOOTNOTES

A work once fully referenced will thereafter be noted either by "ibid" or "op. cit."

CONTENTS

PREFACE: BECOMING A MOUNTAIN-MOVER! 7

CHAPTER ONE: FAITH IS THE VICTORY 15

CHAPTER TWO: WHAT YOU BELIEVE FOR - YOU GET! 25

CHAPTER THREE: YOUR WORD OF FAITH 45

CHAPTER FOUR: SPEAK THE WORD.. 59

CHAPTER FIVE: FAITH IS ESSENTIAL.. 81

CHAPTER SIX: WORDS THAT WORK MIRACLES 99

CHAPTER SEVEN: THE INGREDIENTS OF FAITH 115

CHAPTER EIGHT: THE NATURE OF FAITH 137

CHAPTER NINE: NUGGETS OF FAITH 151

CHAPTER TEN: MORE NUGGETS 169

ABBREVIATIONS

Abbreviations commonly used for the books of the Bible are

Genesis	Ge	Habakkuk	Hb
Exodus	Ex	Zephaniah	Zp
Leviticus	Le	Haggai	Hg
Numbers	Nu	Zechariah	Zc
Deuteronomy	De	Malachi	Mal
Joshua	Js		
Judges	Jg		
Ruth	Ru	Matthew	Mt
1 Samuel	1 Sa	Mark	Mk
2 Samuel	2 Sa	Luke	Lu
1 Kings	1 Kg	John	Jn
2 Kings	2 Kg	Acts	Ac
1 Chronicles	1 Ch	Romans	Ro
2 Chronicles	2 Ch	1 Corinthians	1 Co
Ezra	Ezr	2 Corinthians	2 Co
Nehemiah	Ne	Galatians	Ga
Esther	Es	Ephesians	Ep
Job	Jb	Philippians	Ph
Psalm	Ps	Colossians	Cl
Proverbs	Pr	1 Thessalonians	1 Th
Ecclesiastes	Ec	2 Thessalonians	2 Th
Song of Songs	Ca *	1 Timothy	1 Ti
Isaiah	Is	2 Timothy	2 Ti
Jeremiah	Je	Titus	Tit
Lamentations	La	Philemon	Phm
Ezekiel	Ez	Hebrews	He
Daniel	Da	James	Ja
Hosea	Ho	1 Peter	1 Pe
Joel	Jl	2 Peter	2 Pe
Amos	Am	1 John	1 Jn
Obadiah	Ob	2 John	2 Jn
Jonah	Jo	3 John	3 Jn
Micah	Mi	Jude	Ju
Nahum	Na	Revelation	Re

Ca is an abbreviation of *Canticles*, a derivative of the Latin name of the *Song of Solomon*, which is sometimes also called the *Song of Songs*.

6

PREFACE

BECOMING A MOUNTAIN-MOVER!

The rightness or wrongness of our believing is something we must all face. The Bible warns against the results of wrong believing, and vigorously stresses the importance of right believing. So it is vital for you to learn how to have faith in God, but even more, how to use your faith rightly.

The Bible says: **"Without faith it is impossible to please God, for those who come to God must believe."** Plainly then, if you wish to please God, you must come to him in **faith**. And what is this **faith**? It is a sure confidence that **"God exists, and that he rewards those who diligently seek him"** (He 11:6).

Now this kind of real faith has

LIMITLESS POSSIBILITIES!

Many times the Lord Jesus Christ spoke about the enormous potential of your own faith in God. He said: **"All things are possible if you believe!"** And again: **"Nothing shall be impossible for you!"** And here is a passage of special importance: `Truly, I say to you, if you have faith and never doubt, you will ... say to this mountain, `Be taken up and cast into the sea,' and it will be done. And whatever you ask in prayer, you will receive, if you have faith!" (Mt 21:21- 22).

Notice that Christ did **not** say, "Whatever you ask in **prayer** you will receive;" but, "Whatever you ask in prayer **believing**, you will receive!"

Believing, or **faith**, makes the difference between prayer that moves mountains and prayer that moves nothing. **Faith** is the key that unlocks the power of the all-powerful Christ.

He says, "All power in heaven and on earth has been given to me!" (Mt 28:18). But why does he say it? Just to boast about himself, just to tell us something about his personal glory? Hardly! He speaks rather for **your** benefit, to tell you something about **yourself**, about what you are in him, and about what you can do in his strength. Hence, if Christ does have "all power", it is so that his disciples might "go ... and make ...!" (Mt 28:19-20).

Notice, he does not say, "I have all power, so I will go;" but, "I have all power so that **you** can go!" He is seeking a faith response from you. He says, "I am with you always, I have all power," so that **you** might exclaim with bold faith, **"The Lord is my helper, I will not be afraid; what can man do to me!"** (He 13:5-6).

When he died on the cross, Jesus took upon himself all of our sin, sickness, failure and death. But then through his resurrection he triumphed over all of those foes. And now, since he has defeated our most bitter enemy, death, we know that he is able to conquer every lesser peril that threatens us. There is no sin, or habit, or fear, or disease from which he cannot set us free.

But faith, and faith alone, can bring you into unfailing contact with this awesome ability of Christ. But faith **will** do it. Your own faith **can** bring you the miracle you need. If you have faith you will get your answer. What you believe for you will receive. **Faith** without **result** is as impossible as rain without water, or as sunshine without light.

Faith obtains! Faith possesses! Faith moves the hand of God! Faith captures the divine promise and makes it perform!

AUTHORITY AND DOMINION

God made man, not to be defeated, but to have authority over the whole earth and all that it contains. The Lord said: "Let them have **dominion** ... Fill the earth and **subdue** it, and have **dominion** over it" (Ge 1:26-28).

That decree gave to man power and authority to govern every created thing. All that inhabited the earth was subject to his command - fish, birds, animals, even the natural elements.

Something of what that authority meant was demonstrated by Christ when he walked on the water, hushed a howling storm with a word, fed thousands of people with only a handful of food, rode an untamed colt through a cheering crowd, and so on.

But man sinned. He disobeyed God. The divine mandate was warped. Instead of living as a conqueror, man was conquered. He became enslaved by his own sin. He found himself tyrannised by deserts and jungles, by storms and earthquakes, by wind and flood, by fang and fire, and by infirmity and death.

Being separated from the source of limitless power, man was confined within his own feeble resources. From being the master he was reduced to chains, held in bondage by his own physical limitations, by his fears, and, above all, by the death and judgment that must follow (He 2:15; 9:27).

Through prodigious mechanical and technological effort, man has managed to regain some of his lost dominion. But the larger picture of humanity is still one of a race sick, dying, defeated. And so long as sin and unbelief endure, that scene will remain essentially unaltered.

GOOD NEWS

Despite this sad picture of failure, there is a wonderful way of escape. Christ came to reverse man's bondage, to give us back our dominion, and to restore to us all that sin and Satan had stolen. He did this by giving his life as a ransom for our lives. His death on the cross paid the debt for our sin. And his resurrection has made available to us the immense ability of God to loose us from every fetter, to set us free, and to make us more than conquerors in every conflict.

Potentially, all that Adam lost has been restored to you by Christ - although in practice the realisation of that wealth and power is presently limited to certain specific areas of authority. We cannot fully regain our lost dominion until the coming day of resurrection. But you **can** be sure of having access to invincible strength in every situation that challenges the outworking of God's will in your life.

However, the release of that victory lies in your own faith. **By faith you must lay hold of God's mighty promises and make those promises a reality in your own experience.** As the scripture says, *"This is the victory that overcomes the world, even **our faith**"* (1 Jn 5:4).

By faith you can conquer the "world"! By faith you can regain the control that Adam lost. Faith can give you mastery in every circumstance - either to change that circumstance, or to remain in God's will despite it. Nothing can discourage, or hinder, or defeat, the man or woman who is resolute in faith!

ABUNDANTLY VICTORIOUS

Whatever may be said of the rest of the world, the Christian should be living with strength and triumph. The Bible standard for the believer is this:

> "On that day the Lord will put a shield about (them) ... so that the feeblest among them on that day shall be like David, *and the house of David shall be like God, like the angel of the Lord, at their head*" *(Ze 12:8).*

That is an exciting picture of the great deliverance and defence the Lord offers his people today. It declares that the weakest among them should at least have the strength of a David; and as for the strongest - they should be **like the Angel of the Lord** in authority, confidence, and might!

That is why Paul said, "Be strong in the Lord and in the strength of his might" (Ep 6:10). That is a command, not to **ask** for, but to **accept** strength. Don't ask. Act! By faith accept that "the strength of his might" is already yours through Christ and the indwelling Spirit.

The Lord said, **"I give you authority over all the power of the enemy, and nothing by any means shall hurt you!"** (Lu 10:19-20).

Believe it! Know that you do have dominion. If you are in Christ, then all of the victorious dynamic of his resurrection is yours by right. His triumph over Satan and all his works has become **your** triumph. You can appropriate that victory by faith, and so make it real in your own life.

Mark these tremendous statements: "If God is for us, who can be against us ... we are more than conquerors ... give thanks to God, who always causes us to triumph ... I can do all things in Christ who strengthens me ... strengthened with all might according to his glorious power ... I am complete in him!" (Ro 8:37; 2 Co 2:14; Ph 4:13; Cl 1:11; 2:10)

All of those biblical sayings are true of every believer in Christ. But they will not automatically work for you. They must be called into reality by **faith**. Only you can transform the promise into performance. You must put yourself into the promise, personalise it, and say, "This is true of me!" Your **faith** in the promise is the thing that will bring into your life all of the power that lies in the promise.

NOTHING IS IMPOSSIBLE

Jesus said, "If you have faith, and do not doubt, you can say to a mountain, 'Remove yourself!' and it will move. **Nothing shall be impossible for you**" (cp. Mt 21:21-22; 17:20).

Notice that the invitation is to **say**, not **pray**. There are times when what you **say** is much more important than what you **pray**. There are times when instead of **praying about** the mountains of life, you should be boldly **speaking to** them, with the authority of faith, and commanding them to be removed. The promise of Christ is unequivocal. He stated bluntly: tell the mountain to shift out of the way, and it will shift, so long as you speak with **faith**.

So Jesus asserted that a spoken word of faith would give a believer absolute dominion in every circumstance. Nothing is impossible for those who have learned, not only how to pray, but even more how to **say**! No barrier is insuperable to those who can speak the command of faith!

UNDERGOING OR OVERCOMING

Some people are **undergoers**. Others are **overcomers**. It is **faith** that makes the difference.

Some are swept along by the tides of life. Others, like Jesus, walk on top of those same tides, and are unhurt by them. The difference is **faith**.

Some believe, and please God by their believing. To them is given an abundant supply of heaven's resources. Others are haunted by dreads and doubts. By their lack of faith they are actually calling God a liar (1 Jn 5:9-10). No wonder they receive nothing from the Lord. No wonder the Bible says, "Without faith it is **impossible** to please God."

So stir up your faith. Throw off doubt and unbelief. God will do what he has said he will do. He only waits for you to believe it, and to begin to act accordingly. Dare to believe! Believe for every need! Your believing will do it!

Mark it well: **ALL THINGS ARE POSSIBLE IF YOU BELIEVE!"**

WHY THIS BOOK?

The purpose of the following chapters is to bring you into a new dimension in your understanding of prayer and of the abundant life God has called you to enjoy in Christ.

As the chapters progress you will find some ideas repeated in different ways; ground already covered will be traversed again from a different direction. This repetition is essential if all of the aspects of faith are to be adequately explored.

However, the chapters will advance steadily in their development of the concepts of faith and toward their goal of showing you not only the **doctrine** of faith, but more importantly its **dynamic**. For faith is perhaps the one thing where doctrine by itself is utterly sterile. Merely to learn about faith is vacuity. Faith must be **practised**. It must act. **"Faith without works,"** said James, **"is dead"** (Ja 2:17).

So it is my prayer that the result of your studies will be a new explosion of faith in your life.

Finally, I would like to acknowledge a personal debt to the late Pastor Leo C. Harris, the founder of the CRC Churches International in Australia. Many of the faith concepts that are now completely my own were first planted 30 years ago in my spirit by him. His life and ministry were a constant example of the principles of faith in action. He lived what he taught. Even the title of this course *Faith Dynamics* was suggested by a group of studies that he presented to his congregation in Adelaide. I have made use of notes from those studies in a few places in this book. However, resemblance to the original is now fairly remote. Which is only to say that I alone must accept the blame for any deficiencies you may find here.

Now may God gain glory from the miracle of **his** faith born in **your** spirit!

CHAPTER ONE

FAITH IS THE VICTORY

Like a man with a headache (he doesn't want to get rid of his head, but it hurts him to keep it) many people find that Christianity is a problem. They can't afford to throw it away, because they know it is their only guarantee of eternal life. Yet Christian life is a real burden to them. They are undergoing rather than overcoming, enduring rather than enjoying, existing rather than truly living in the abundant blessing of God.

The problem lies in their failure to overcome the world - on the contrary, they are overcome by the world. And for this there is only one answer: the victory faith brings (1 Jn 5:4).

What is "the world"? What is this "faith" that can give us mastery over it?

THE WORLD

When John talks about the "world" he does not mean the physical earth made by God, which is very good (Ge 1:31). That "world" is not your enemy. Scripture says: "The earth is the Lord's, and the fulness thereof ... every beast of the forest is his, and the cattle upon a thousand hills ... the silver is his, and the gold is his." The entire physical creation belongs to God, and he has given it to his own people to enjoy. Everything God has made is "yours" - to use for your own pleasure and prosperity, as well as for his glory (Ps 24:1; Ps 50:10-12;1 Co 3:21-23; 3 Jn 2).

Away then with the pernicious idea that there is something evil in this good old earth fashioned by the hand of the Lord. Above all people, Christians should enjoy living in their Father's world!

But there is another "world" that is antagonistic to God and his church - the "world" fashioned by men, corrupted by sin, and ruled by Satan. It is the "world" (as Jesus said) that "loves darkness rather than light." It has the devil as its "prince", and it hates the children of God "because they are not of the *world*." This is the fallen "world" of human society and government; and in particular, that part of human society that is distinct from the kingdom of God and foreign to the will of God.

This "world" presents a five-fold opposition to the Christian:
1. it opposes us spiritually, by saying that there is no God and by mocking the reality of heaven;
2. it opposes us morally, by inciting us to lustful rebellion against God;
3. it opposes us intellectually, by challenging the validity of our faith, and by scorning the scriptures;
4. it opposes us physically, by inflicting disease, poverty, and fear; and
5. it opposes us socially, through constant persecutions.

But against the apparent enormity of this world's strength, we can lift up one invincible weapon, even ....

OUR FAITH

What is the character of this faith that overcomes the world? Where does it come from? How should it be exercised?

Faith Is Not An Option

The general rule is that nothing will be done for us other than what we truly believe for. You can usually gain from God only what unwavering and confident faith requires him to do.

Jesus showed this in his strong word to the woman of Canaan. He said, *"Woman, great is your faith! Let it be done for you as you desire"* (Mt 15:28). How determined the woman was that Jesus would heal her daughter! Now such determination alone would not have moved the Lord; but when Christ saw that her determination was coupled with faith, thus creating what Jesus called great faith, he did for her exactly what she wanted.

He will do for you "exactly as you desire" if you too display the same great faith. And you <u>can</u> show such faith! If that humble woman from Canaan, uninstructed in the ways of the Lord, lacking many advantages that you have, could find great faith in God, so too can you!

On another occasion, a man cried out in desperation for the Lord to heal his son. Jesus did not immediately answer his prayer. The Lord's first concern was to instruct the man to believe - he said: "If you can! All things are possible to him who believes" (Mk 9:23). Here was a straightforward challenge indeed! Into the face of the man's desperate need, into his broken heart, the Lord hurled this stern rebuke, this ringing call to the man's own faith. Some would have been offended by Jesus' response, and would have gone away angry and unheard. But out of his passionate love for his son, this father found courage equal to the occasion: "Immediately," the scripture says, "the father of the child cried out and said, `I believe; help my unbelief!'" Christ was thrilled by that passionate faith-response. It drew from him a powerful command that drove the devil out of the boy and healed him completely.

That kind of faith is as effective now as it was then; it will move the compassion of Christ now, as it did then. Dare to believe! To believe for every need! Your believing will do it! Mark it well. "All things are possible to him who believes!"

What is the response in your heart as you hear that mighty word of the Lord? Does your prayer leap forth in eager expectancy? Or does your heart remain dull? Listen to the Lord speak again, and hear the beat of your heart, and know whether you need to do something about unbelief -

"ALL THINGS ARE POSSIBLE TO HIM WHO BELIEVES!"

Everybody Has Faith

When I say that "everybody has faith", I mean that each person has a potential ability to believe God. We all have a capacity for faith. Everyone is born with this capacity, and everyone makes use of it in some part of daily life. The fact that you have faith is proved by the fact that you have fear. Fear, when it becomes an overpowering, controlling force, is faith perverted.

There is of course a legitimate fear. It is the natural emotion that arises from your sense of self-preservation, giving you an inward warning of actual danger. But fear goes astray if it takes possession of you, and torments you. When that happens fear has mastered your capacity for faith, and has perverted your faith to an overpowering belief that evil will certainly overtake you. When fear is thus allowed to dominate you, it bends the powerful force of your natural faith into a deep dread that will ultimately destroy you. The natural emotion of fear is intended to tell you that danger lies ahead; but once that warning has been given, it is then time for FAITH to take control of the situation and to trust God for a way of escape.

God gave you this ability to believe so that you might direct it toward him, and place your confidence in his power and provision. The Lord has always endeavored to guide people to live by the power of an abiding faith. But the great enemies of this faith are fear and doubt. Jesus said: "You must have faith, and do not doubt" ... (Mk11:22-23). Likewise James: "Ask in faith and do not waver" ... (1:6). Hence faith must be purged of all doubt and all wavering before it can become effective. Great faith is that faith in which there is no element of doubt, no uncertainty, no hesitancy. But if those things are present in your believing, and so overshadow your faith, then it may be said that you have only "little faith", or even "no faith".

For example, in one time of danger, when the disciples were panic stricken, Jesus rebuked them and sternly asked, "Where is your faith?" They had faith, but somewhere in the turmoil of their fear it had become "lost" - that is, it was no longer effective. Their faith, paralysed by fear, was powerless to help them (Lu 8:22-25).

What is this faith that the disciples could have used to still the wild ocean? The Bible says that faith is the evidence of things not seen.

It is an ability to reach beyond ourselves, to go past the obvious circumstances that surround us. It is a capacity to be convinced of the reality of things that are not yet visible. It enables us to anticipate things that are not yet perceptible to the natural senses. Faith is the outreach of the human heart to God, an outreach based on unwavering confidence in the integrity of God's Word and in his ability and power to meet every need, to overcome every situation.

When that outreach of faith is maintained without doubt or double-mindedness, then God declares that he is compelled to respond to it in power. This is great faith. This is faith that moves mountains. This is faith that changes the appearance of things. This real faith refuses to be influenced by anything heard, seen, or felt, but rather itself influences those things and forces them into conformity with its own irresistible dictate!

So then, let me say it again: everybody can have faith; but the determining factor is the way in which you use your faith.

Faith Born In Prayer

Oliver Cromwell was one of the most remarkable military leaders in English history. Many reasons have been advanced to explain his extraordinary success. But historians have generally overlooked what was certainly one of the chief factors in his triumph: before embarking on any campaign Cromwell and his officers spent many hours, and sometimes days, in prayer before God, looking for what they quaintly called "a door of hope." They meant, a deep heaven-inspired conviction that God was with them, and an unwavering confidence that they would be victorious. It was faith born in prayer. And it guaranteed their ultimate success!

Have you ever wondered why Christ spent so much time in prayer? It was not that he lacked anything. But I suggest that through prayer he was seeking to invigorate his faith - to make it active, powerful, irresistible. Then with this prayer-born faith he went out to heal the sick, hush the storm, multiply the loaves and fishes, and to show himself master of all that was in the world.

> *"Men ought always to pray, and not to faint,"!*
> *(Lu 18:1-8). said Christ.*

Thus showing that the greatest function of prayer is to create faith, so that we may not be weak, but strong, and may gloriously overcome the world

Now it may be thought that this idea of faith arising out of prayer contradicts what I have said just above about everybody possessing faith. However, it must be recognised that faith is both a natural attribute of the human spirit and a divine impulse. In a Christian setting, faith is truly effective only as its motivating power comes from the touch of God. In other words, a distinction must be made between faith as it is exercised by ungodly people in ordinary life, and faith as it is exercised by Christians toward God and his promise.

There does seem to be a natural law of faith, which can be utilised by anyone anywhere in all kinds of circumstances. It functions as impartially and as surely as any other natural law - say, the law of gravity. Anyone who masters the principles that govern this natural attribute of faith can operate it successfully, and be enriched by it. Scores of books on "positive thinking" show how truly this law of faith has been appropriated by great numbers of prosperous people in our world. I do not think it would be an exaggeration to say that underlying every successful enterprise in modern commercial life you could find a proper use of this law of faith.

But that natural attribute of faith can be used without divine assistance. It may lead people away from God as readily as toward him. The fact is faith, as the Bible understands it, is always more than just a natural attribute. In a Christian setting, faith cannot exist apart from the enlivening touch of God. Hence the Bible tells us that faith is a gift of the Holy Spirit, and also a fruit of the Spirit. The Christian is required to live in the anointing of the Holy Spirit, and to "walk in the Spirit" day by day so that his faith will be continually nourished and strengthened. For a Christian, the great purpose of faith is to enable him to do the will of God. He wants faith for no other reason, or at least for no greater reason.

Faith is a necessary part of obedience. Not one of us can realise the full potential of God's purpose for us, nor can we understand the true nature of his good promise, without his assistance. Only a divine impulse can open our eyes. Only the touch of God can impart to our faith the quality that makes it invincible against all the opposition of the world. Hence Paul wrote:

> *"I pray that ... God ... may give you a spirit of wisdom and of revelation in the knowledge of him, having the eyes of your heart enlightened, that you may know ... what is the immeasurable greatness of his power in us who believe" (Ep 1:16-21; see also Col 1:9,11).*

You may believe, but unless God opens your eyes, imparts to you a divine revelation of who and what you are in him, and infuses into you the dynamic of his Holy Spirit, your faith will be unable to rise above a natural level. So your own natural faith is worthless to God, except for the foundation it provides upon which, by the Holy Spirit, he can build the true Christian grace of faith.

I have said that faith is both a fruit and a gift of the Holy Spirit.

It Is A Fruit Of The Spirit (Ga 5:22)

This indicates that your capacity for faith can be constantly enlarged as you live under the influence of the Spirit. Faith should become an increasingly prominent part of your experience, its exploits should be more pronounced, it should grow to be an outstanding characteristic of your Christian experience.

Such Spirit-directed faith will focus more and more upon discovering what things God wants you to do, what kind of person he wants you to be, what things he wants to happen to you, and it will cause those things to be realised. If the call of God is for public greatness, faith will enable you to achieve it. If the call of God is for public obscurity, faith will enable you to embrace it.

Whatever is of divine provenance, faith (and only faith) can bring to proper fruition in your life - whether prosperity or paucity, strength or weakness, health or infirmity, greatness or littleness, life or death.

Without faith, Spirit-inspired, prayer-born, God-illuminated, faith, we cannot begin to do the will of God nor to receive his promise. The things of the world may be accessible to natural faith; but the things of the Spirit - that is, those things, whatever they are, that encompass the will of God for your life - can be comprehended and embraced only by Spirit-quickened faith.

It Is A Gift Of The Spirit (1 Co 12:9)

This idea of a "gift" indicates that when you suddenly find yourself faced with a great mountain of difficulty, or threatened by an exigency for which your ordinary resources (even of faith) are hopelessly inadequate, then you can swiftly draw on the resources of the Holy Spirit and gain an immediate inflow of heaven's faith!

Christ described the same principle when he said:

> *"Have the faith of God. Truly I say to you, whoever says to this mountain, `Be taken up and cast into the sea,' and does not doubt in his heart, but believes that what he says will come to pass, it will be done for him" (Mk 11:22-23; lit.)*[1]

---

[1] The Greek construction used here is called an objective genitive. It occurs several times in the NT. Its ordinary translation, and surface meaning, is objective, not genitive; thus, "have faith in (or towards) God." Why then use the genitive case ("of God"), and not the normal accusative or dative? The purpose is to show that God is not only the object of faith, but also the source of it.

This is a common Greek construction, to use the genitive case to show that the object of a sentiment or action, is also the source or occasion of its existence.

It occurs in the following:

None of us can be sufficiently rid of doubt to have that kind of mountain-moving faith unless God gives it to us to believe.

No one in fact, can exercise faith at all, in a Christian setting, beyond what God has determined for his or her life.

This must be so; for Christian faith has such limitless possibilities, as big as God himself, that it must be confined to the limits of God's will for each person.

Our responsibility, under the direction of the Holy Spirit, is to discover the things that require faith from each one of us personally, and then to set ourselves to believe for those things, and no others. To try to exercise faith for anything that lies outside of God's purpose is to step from faith into presumption - which is a certain way to ruin.

But let faith flourish in your heart as both a gift and fruit of the Holy Spirit, let that faith wax mighty on the strength of a promise from God, and truly nothing will be impossible for you!"

"the faith of Jesus Christ" (Ga 2:16, twice) = faith in Christ, but also indicates that Christ is the sole author of saving faith. - "the prayer of God (Lu 6:12) = prayer to God, but shows also that only the living God can inspire true prayer.

"the reproach of Christ" (He 11:26) = abuse suffered for Christ, but points also to the fact that these sufferings arise from his will for us.

"the conscience of God" (1 Pe 2:19) = because of conscience toward God, but acknowledges also that a good conscience is his gift;

"the love of God" (Jn 5:42) = love for God, but shows also that we love him only as he himself inspires that love. If we have love for God, we must first receive love from him; it is of him before it can be to him - see also Ro 5:5; 2 Th. 3:5; 1 Jn. 2:5, 15. And what is true of spiritual grace of love is equally true of faith.

CHAPTER TWO

WHAT YOU BELIEVE FOR - YOU GET!

"As you have believed, so it will be done for you!"
(Mt 8:13)

"AS ... SO!"

There is no way of escaping that irresistible law. It binds you to itself as surely as gravity binds you to the earth. It is a law of God. Immutable. Irreversible. You will get what you believe for. According to the way you believe, so it will happen. Your **believing** will determine what is done in your life.

From this universal law, certain propositions can be drawn...

FAITH

CHRIST IS LOOKING FOR FAITH

AS you believe **SO** it will be done. The doing is determined by your believing. You will receive what you believe to receive. God is all-powerful; Jesus Christ is the same yesterday, today, and forever; **but your needs will be met only according to your believing!**

People try to put the responsibility onto God for the miracles they need. But the scriptures are emphatic: the responsibility for answered prayer is almost entirely ours. The point at issue is not what **God** can **do** but what can **you** believe?

If you can believe, you **will** receive!

See how forcibly Christ places the onus on the person who is praying:

*"Whatever **you** desire, when you pray, **believe that you receive** and you will receive!". And again: "As*

you have believed, so it will be done for you!" (Mk 11:23-24)

To the man who wondered whether or not Christ could help him, the Master retorted, "The question is not, 'Can **I** help you?' but, 'Can **you** believe?' All things are possible to him who believes!" (see Mk 9:20-23).

This man had said to Jesus, "If you **can** do anything, please help us!" But Jesus at once turned the challenge back to him: "If **you** can **believe**..."

Yes, if you can believe it, God will do it! The key factor is not God's ability - for God can do anything - **but your believing**.

There is little value in pleading, "God, help me if you can!" The answer will be returned from heaven, "Of course I can help you; but can **you** believe?" In this matter, the "if" does not belong with God, but with man. There is no uncertainty about what God can do; but there may well be uncertainty about what you can believe!

We cannot evade this responsibility. The decree of God is irrevocable. He demands faith. "Without faith it is impossible to please him." Whoever comes to God **"must** believe." Whatever need you may have, the admonition is urgent:

> *"Ask God, who gives to all men generously... **But ask in faith**, with no doubting, for he who doubts is like a wave of the sea that is driven and tossed by the wind... Such a double-minded man, unstable in all his ways, will not receive anything from the Lord" (Ja 1:5-7).*

Open your minds to this divine law. Understand it. Accept it. You cannot escape it. **As you have believed, so it will be done for you."**

ACTIVE FAITH

It is not possible to remain uncommitted in this matter of the way you use your faith. Look into your own heart and you will find that

right now you are believing something. God has given you an ability to believe and you are using this ability every hour of the day.

Think about it this way. God has given you eyes, and you cannot help but see; he has given you ears, and you cannot help but hear. In the same manner he has given you the power to believe, **and you cannot help but believe!**

But just as you can control the faculties of sight and hearing so you can control this faith-faculty. You can look and listen in a way that will enrich your whole life, and open your soul to God; or you can misuse God's gifts and bring destruction upon yourself.

So with your capacity for faith. You can believe rightly or wrongly. The exercise of your believing power can take you toward God or away from him. How are you believing right now? Toward God or Satan? To get well or to stay sick? To succeed or fail? Are you trusting in the word of God, or in the knowledge of your senses?

Whatever you are believing you will get, for your believing is always productive. "As you believe, so will you receive." This law remains operative whether your believing is right or wrong, in harmony with God's purpose or against it. This leads to three important ideas ...

Wrong Believing Is What The Bible Calls Unbelief

It is vital to realise that "unbelief" is not so much "**non-**believing" as it is "**wrong-**believing". Unbelievers are actually believing, but they are believing wrongly. That is, their belief is directed away from God and away from the promise of God. They believe a witness other than the witness of God's word. Instead, they believe the testimony that the godless world conveys to them, the testimony of the kingdom of darkness, the witness of their natural senses, the arguments of those who hate God, and who have rejected his word.

So their belief separates them **from** God, it does not attach them **to** him. But that belief is nonetheless powerful. It has a resultant harvest as irresistible as that which springs from the seed of faith planted by the righteous. "Wrong" believing, or unbelief, finds its inevitable product in isolation from God, in sin and sickness, and ultimately in total death.

Unbelief attracts those things that belong to the kingdom of darkness as surely as true belief attracts those things that belong to the kingdom of God!

Right Believing Is What The Bible Calls Faith

"Faith" is the name given to your believing power when it is directed toward God. You have faith when you believe that God exists, and that he will generously and graciously do for you all that he has promised to do. So if the Bible says, "Repent, and trust in Christ, and God will pardon all your sin and give you eternal life," then we expect that it shall be so. If the Bible says, "They shall lay hands on the sick and they shall recover," then we expect that God will do it. If the Bible promises us personal victory, or an abundant supply of all that we need, or a glorious hope in Christ's return, we look for those things to be done. That is right-believing, or faith.

Abraham was a man who knew how to believe God in the face of overwhelming difficulties (Ro 4:19-21). God had promised him a son, Isaac, but both Abraham and his wife were now very old, and it was humanly and naturally impossible for them to have a child. What then was Abraham to believe? Was he to believe in the physical impossibility of a son being born to him and Sarah? Or should he believe the promise of God?

If he had allowed himself to be influenced by natural considerations alone, he would have been guilty of **wrong-believing** (unbelief), because he would have been believing contrary to God's word.

But faith is a conviction that God is not a liar; a deep conviction that he will perform what he has promised; an unwavering assurance that God will unfailingly respond to trust in his word.

So it was with Abraham: "In the presence of the God in whom he believed, who gives life to the dead and calls into existence the things that do not exist...**he did not weaken in faith** when he considered his own body, which was as good as dead... no distrust made him waver concerning the promise of God, but he grew strong in his faith as he gave glory to God, **fully convinced that God was able to do what he had promised.**"

Abraham provides a wonderful demonstration of right believing. He proved himself to be a man who had his believing power under control. If you and I would tap the supernatural resources of God, we also **must** get our believing under control.

In response to the truth that "all things are possible to him who believes" (Mk 9:23) you must compel your faith to be directed towards God and his promise; you must force your believing away from the consideration of (belief in) things that are contrary to God's word; you must determine to believe only what God says, and to insist that every word of his good promise to you be richly fulfilled. That is right believing. That is **faith**.

The possibilities of right believing are as unlimited as the promise and power of God. Positive faith in God will bring you into dynamic connection with all of heaven's inexhaustible ability to meet your every need. It will bring you into co-operation with the Lord.

When you have faith you take God's view of things. You think, speak, and act as he would, reckoning that all the resources of heaven are at your command. Positive believing (faith) gives access to heaven's limitless supply of all your needs, whether they are spiritual, physical, material, emotional, or financial.

It Takes The Same Energy To Believe Rightly As To Believe Wrongly

Whether your believing power is channelled negatively or positively, the same effort is required. The only things altered are the direction of your believing and its results. Fear, anxiety, stress, worry, are all signs of negative believing. Faith, trust, peace, confidence are signs of positive believing.

Most people find it easier to believe wrongly; not because it is actually difficult to believe positively, but because they have developed a habit of wrong believing. This habit is a product of the inroads of sin into human life. The sinful habits of many years are hard to break! But we Christians have an answer to this - the Cross, where the "old man" with all of his ways is put to death, and we are clothed with the "new man" who reflects the image of Christ. (2Co 5:17)

For us, then, whether we believe rightly or wrongly is now a matter of choice. In Christ you **can** choose to discard all of your old patterns of believing and begin to believe rightly; that is, to exercise **faith**.

FAITH / FEAR
LOOKING OUT OR LOOKING UP?

The greatest enemy of faith is fear. In the scriptures, faith is contrasted more often with fear than with any other thing. Nearly one hundred times the injunction is found: "fear not", "do not be afraid"; and the same idea is expressed another hundred times in different words. And in almost every place the command not to be afraid is associated with encouragement to have faith in God.

Fear is a destructive force. The apostle acknowledged this when he wrote, **"Fear contains its own punishment"** (1 Jn 4:18, lit.)[2] - it carries a penalty, it creates the very pain it fears. In the words of the old version, "fear hath torment" - torment of soul and spirit, torment of mind and body.

Our hospitals, sanatoriums, and asylums are filled with stark evidence of the truth of that statement. Jesus drew attention to the

---

[2] There is an ambiguity in John's original statement. Some translators and commentators refer the passage to the last judgment - that final punishment of God upon all sin, including the sin of fear. Thus, several translations read: "Fear has to do with **punishment**." But John's use of the present tense - "fear **has** torment" - seems to require the sense I have given in this Chapter, without excluding the idea that those who cling to their fears may eventually be excluded from the kingdom (Re 21:8). The NEB rather cleverly includes both ideas (present pain and future punishment) in its translation of the passage: "Fear brings with it the **pains** of **judgment**" (emphasis mine).

same problem when he spoke about "men fainting with fear" because all of their attention is gripped by "what is coming upon the world" (Lu 21:26). Their expectation is directed toward what is about to happen on earth instead of toward God. They are looking at the wrong thing, they are looking in the wrong way, they are looking in the wrong direction.

Notice, it is not the events themselves that cause people to fear; rather, it is their **attitude** toward those events. They live in dread of what is about to happen. They are filled with an uneasy foreboding. They live in fearful anticipation of coming trouble. Fear that has torment, fear that causes men's hearts to fail, comes from looking into the future and being afraid that the worst will happen. It is an anticipation of disaster. These people see only darkness, threat, and peril; they do not recognise the goodness of God, they have no real trust in his providence, they live in anxiety about tomorrow, burdened with the worry of what they believe lies before them.

But notice that Christ described another group of people, who are living alongside the first, but with this difference: the former are "looking out" and are afraid; the latter are "looking up" and are filled with faith! (vs. 28). Fear does not arise so much from surrounding conditions as it does from our outlook, that is, from our attitude towards those conditions.

The disciples looked out at the storm, and they were terrified; Jesus looked up to the Father and with calm confidence hushed the wind and the seas. Then he rebuked the disciples for their fear. In his opinion they could offer no excuse for so readily surrendering their faith (Mk 4:35-41).

So the main difference between faith and fear is the **direction** in which they are bent. The one thrusts into the disasters, perplexities, anxieties, distresses, and troubles that come into human life - and it is broken down by the weight of those things. The other thrusts upward to God, rising on the wings of his promise, and finds that "underneath are the everlasting arms", and that the Lord is a strong refuge and defense (De 33:27).

People who are governed by faith fear no evil, but believe only in God's unfailing goodness and mercy.

Deliverance From Fear

I have shown you that every human being has an ability to believe. It was God's intention that people should use this ability to believe in him, and in his promise. But most people have reversed the direction of their believing. Instead of their capacity to believe becoming faith in the unlimited power and resources of God, it has become fear in the negative and destructive forces of Satan.

When man disobeyed God, when he believed the devil's lie, when he was cast out of God's presence, his ability to believe became perverted and misdirected. The faith that was to bring him to God's power and provision became directed into the confused darkness of his own fallen nature. He fell under the tyranny of sin and weakness, and became subject to all the evil that Satan could inflict.

Faith went into reverse and became fear. Fear is man's believing directed toward the works of Satan, whereas it should be directed toward the works of God. But through the grace of God in Christ we can reverse this wrongful tendency and change our deepest expectations away from the crooked pathways of fear into the confident highway of faith. Our song then becomes that of the Psalmist:

> *"For God alone my soul waits with confidence;* **all of my expectation is from him**; *he alone is my rock and my salvation, my fortress; I shall not be moved away;... on God rests my deliverance and my honor; my mighty rock, my refuge, is God"* (see Ps 62:1-2;7-8).

Here is a fact: **fear and faith are both a matter of expectation**. The difference between them lies only in the thing expected. Fear anticipates disaster, whereas faith anticipates triumph. Which of these two will govern your life is a matter of personal choice. Fear and faith both find their beginning in the thing you choose to anticipate.

If you choose to expect the worst, **fear will flourish**, and your expectation of disaster will be strengthened and enlarged. Fear feeds and grows on itself.

If you choose to expect the best, **faith will flourish**, and your expectation of good things will be enhanced and enlivened. A positive expectation provides an impetus for faith that will wax stronger and bolder as you fix your confidence in the good promise of God.

That fear and faith are a matter of personal choice is evident from the imperative, **"Fear not, believe only!"** That is a command to do two things:

Stop fearing and start believing. Implicit in this command is an assumption that you can and should have both of these matters under your own control. The Lord does not require you to do what you cannot do.

If he says, "Fear not!" then it lies in your power to stop being afraid.

If he says, "Believe only!" then it lies in your power to start believing.

The choice is yours!

God will help you to stop being afraid when you **choose** not to be afraid any more. He will help you to believe when you **choose** to take a stand in faith. It begins with your choice. He cannot help you to stop fearing and to start believing until you choose to cast aside your fears and to live by faith alone.

The psalmist showed his understanding of these things when he said (in the passage quoted just above), **"all of my expectation is from him."** His anticipatory powers were under control and directed toward God alone. He expected to receive nothing except what came to him as God's gift. Fear (the anticipation of evil) had no place in his heart.

The Hebrew word translated "expectation" is interesting. It comes from a root that means "to twist together", and it describes a rope, a binding, or an attachment. So the sense is one of being intertwined through the power of expectation to the very thing you expect. Your expectation is like a line with a hook on its end, which you are casting toward an unseen object. It is probable that the hook will find its target, firmly attach itself, and then draw you and the thing you anticipate together - whether that thing is pleasant or unpleasant!

In which direction are you casting your expectation? Is fear attaching you to the thing you dread? Or is faith attaching you to the promise of God?

I hope that you are singing with the psalmist, "**All of my expectation is from God!**"

Solomon sets the same principle before us in this profound statement:

> *"Keep your heart with all diligence, for out of it flow the issues of life" (Pr 4:23).*

The issues of life!

That is, the way your life is shaped; the things it will result in; the outcome of your days - those things are not determined so much by your outer circumstances as by your inner thoughts. **What takes place in your heart is more powerful in shaping your destiny than any happening outside you!**

People commonly blame fate for their misfortune, or they blame their situation, or the deeds of other people - but the real determinant is their own heart. The way you think is the most important factor in shaping what happens to you. Perhaps not from day to day, but certainly in the ultimate issues of your life.

No doubt it is true that any one of us may experience many vicissitudes in life, often caused by factors beyond our control. But if you can learn how to keep your heart with all diligence, maintaining a positive expectation, refusing to surrender to fear, steadily anticipating the goodness and mercy of God, then the eventual outcome will be all that you could desire!

"Fear Not, Believe Only"

Jesus used that terse statement to show people how to switch from wrong believing to right believing, from believing in the negative power of Satan to believing in the positive power of God.[3]

People who ask, "How can I have faith in God?" would never think of asking, "How can I fear evil?" But unhappily, most of us do find it easier to fear (believe in) the worst than to trust in the Lord. How difficult we find it to expect from God the best that he can do; yet we are quite ready to expect from Satan the worst that he can do!

Yet in reality, the former expectation is simply faith in forward motion, while the latter is faith in reverse.

Fear, like faith, has power to attract and produce. Just as faith is the substance of things desired (He 11:1), so fear is the substance of things dreaded.

Job, to his sorrow, discovered the attracting power of fear, and he sadly confessed:

> *"The thing that I fear comes upon me, and what I dread befalls me" (3:25).*

He learned that his fears had power to materialize. Fear attracts the thing dreaded, just as faith attracts the thing desired. This is because fear and faith use the same believing energy; they function in accordance with the same universal principles.

Look at it this way. There is just one law of gravity. It can be either used or abused, thus saving life or destroying it. Hence, a scientist can utilise the force of gravity to hold a satellite in orbit; but a suicide might depend upon the same force to end his life. The force

---

[3] This section and the next are based on a pamphlet by Leo Harris, "Deliverance From Fear." The material is used by permission.

itself, and the laws by which it operates, remain unchanged. It continues to work impartially and irresistibly. But its effect on human life can be radically altered by the way in which people handle it.

The same principles apply to the use of your inborn believing power. That power has the same force, no matter which way you direct it. By it you can bring yourself to destruction or to a more abundant life. What effect it will have on you depends entirely upon how you choose to use it.

That is why Jesus said you should switch from **fear** (negative believing) to **faith** (positive believing). He meant that the same energy, the same effort, the same ability that you would use to fear the worst you should now use to begin anticipating the best. Your believing power should be brought under control and turned in the direction God has always intended it should go.

Consider the following comparison between fearing and believing. Turn to the table of scriptures on the next page, and read them. You should then read them in their full context in your Bible ....

'Fear not' ....'Believe only' (Lu 8:50)

'I shall not want'...........'The Lord is my Shepherd' (Ps 23)

'I will fear no evil'...........'Thou art with me' (Ps 23)

'Whom shall I fear'...........'The Lord is my light' (Ps 27)

'You did not receive a spirit of slavery, to fall back into fear'...........'You have received the Spirit of sonship' (Ro 8:15)

'God has not given us a spirit of fear'...........'But of power, love, and a sound mind' (2 Ti 1:7)

'Fear has torment'...........'Perfect love casts out all fear' (1Jn 4:18)

'Fear not'...........'Believe only, and you will be made whole' (Lu 8:50)

The list could be greatly extended; but it is enough to demonstrate the contrasting powers of fearing and believing, the one leading to ruin, the other to redemption.

Unmask Your Fears

We see then that your God-given ability to anticipate the unseen or unknown must be recognised and then **re**-directed and rightly expressed as faith in God. Otherwise it will be **mis**-directed and wrongly expressed as fear of evil.

One of the key factors in this process is to expose ruthlessly all of your fears. Everything you fear must be mercilessly identified, uncovered, brought out into the light. You cannot fear and believe at the same time. If you have surrendered to one you cannot be controlled by the other. You must make a choice here. It is a matter of your own will

Fear thrives on deceit. This deceit is sometimes so deep-rooted that people often fail to recognize it. They are blinded to the fear that is sapping their health and strength. Perhaps they are unwilling to admit even to themselves that they have fear. Or they give it another name: they excuse it as a natural characteristic, a personality trait, "something I was born with." Thus they justify their fears, and fail to take any action to be rid of them.

So unmask your fears! You will never find a full release in faith until with complete honesty you search out and root out every fear. Give fear its true color, and then turn from it to believe God!

While such fear remains an invited guest in your spirit, faith will be paralysed. You can fear, or you can believe - but you cannot do both together! One or the other will govern you and determine the issues of your life!

People fear many things: death, poverty, loss of employment, failure, sin, their neighbors, fire, water, disease, and on and on. Of course, there is a fear of these things that is natural and proper, the kind of fear that simply leads one to be cautious, and to take whatever steps are necessary to preserve health and happiness. That kind of fear will not negate faith, for it comes into existence only in the presence of actual danger, and it leads to positive action to secure safety.

But there is another kind of fear, one that seizes part of a person's emotional and spiritual life, and that works continually, reaching out in anticipation of hurt or failure, drawing to itself the thing feared. This a fear that dominates, paralyses, inhibits, torments, sees danger where there is none, has no rational base, needs no cause except itself, and is utterly against the promise of God. It is what the Bible calls "a spirit of fear", unhealthy and destructive. You were not born with it. It does not come from God (2 Ti 1:7). It does not belong to you. It has its origin in that father of lies, Satan.

Some Examples

Here are some of the forms fear takes in various people. Perhaps you will identify yourself here. In each of these cases you should notice that three things tend to occur:

- firstly, fear undermines personal confidence and strength, places a restraint on its victims, inhibits freedom of action, and so leads to its own fulfillment;
- secondly, fear creates an opportunity for Satan to seize the advantage, and to create the thing feared;
- thirdly, fear seems to be justified by its fulfillment; so its grip becomes more firm, which creates an even stronger likelihood of the dreaded thing happening again, which makes the fear still worse... and so on to destruction.

Here now are some of the kinds of fear I have encountered over many years of ministry. As you read them, remember that they all have in themselves a power of self-fulfillment. In the end, you get what you expect!

> A man is prosperous, but continually anxious that his wealth will be lost. He becomes a miser, which is worse than being destitute; or else his self-

confidence is so eroded that he becomes incapable of managing his affairs wisely, and so falls into ruin.

A man is healthy, but always dreading sickness, and he so enfeebles himself that he becomes prey to any illness.

A woman is terrified every time she hears an ambulance or police siren, and she is slowly driven to a nervous collapse.

A person has such a dread of car accidents that the angels of God are driven away, and the devil is given an opening to work disaster.[4]

Another yields to influences and forces in his personal makeup, saying that he cannot combat heredity, but forgetting that there is a greater law of life in Christ.

An unhappy experience with debt has made a woman afraid of banks, to the point where she is terrified to enter one, so she becomes a slave to her fear and open to further financial distress.

Here is a man who has such an anticipation of bad news that he feels sick every time the phone rings, or the postman comes, or there is a knock at his door. His fear is irrational, but it fills his life with misery.

There are people who have allowed a good sense of hygiene to become perverted into such a fear of dirt that they cannot bear to shake another person's hand, or to sit at another's table, or to sleep in a strange bed. They become pitiful prisoners of their own fear.

---

[4] I do not mean that every accident has its roots in fear. Even the fearless Paul suffered shipwreck and other misfortunes. Nonetheless, fear can be a cause of accidents, while faith can be a preventative.

Some are afraid of losing the affections of those they love, or of not being accepted by their neighbors and friends. Their fear arouses the very rejection they dread.

People are afraid of open spaces, or of closed spaces, of insects, of fire, of water, of airplanes, of silence, of noise, of heights, of depths, of dogs, of cats, of other people, of living, and of dying....

There are countless paranoias, some more severe than others, but all of them possessing a measure of torment and of ability to attract the thing feared. People who yield to such fears condemn themselves every day to bondage.

Those fears, each one of them, all of them, must be pulled out of the shadows, exposed to open scrutiny, and recognised for what they are. They can no longer be excused or justified. Hound them out of their hiding places; confess them as sin; place them under the precious blood; banish them in the name of Jesus, so that your faith may be free to turn fully to God and to seize his mighty blessing!

Panic Not!

There is another sort of fear, the kind of fear that was the actual reason for Christ's admonition, "Fear not, believe only!" The frightened person was a father horrified by the news of his daughter's death (Lu 8:40-42, 49-56). The fear in this case is the kind of **panic-reaction** that is likely to overwhelm us when we are confronted by a sudden crisis or peril.

Christ observed the man's terror and at once gave him a word from heaven, a divine revelation, **"She shall be well!"** Then, on the strength of that promise, Christ insisted that the man should master his fear and bring all of his faith-resources together into one all-powerful act of believing that would prove to be even stronger than death. The effectiveness of the promise depended upon the man doing this. If he failed to do it, if he allowed fear to run rampant in his soul, then an impassable barrier would be erected against the healing power of Christ, and his daughter would grow cold in death.

The man seized the opportunity. He accepted the promise of deliverance Jesus had spoken. He drove panic away. He believed. And his daughter was made whole!

That story displays the two best antidotes to fears of every sort, whether paranoias, phobias, deep-seated anxieties, persistent dreads, or quick panic. The remedy remains the same. It is simply this: **the word of God, and an awareness of the presence of Christ.** If you know that the Master is with you, if you have discovered a word from God that opposes your pain then you have all you need to banish every fear, to believe only, and to receive the good things God has promised you!

Why Do People Cling To Their Fears?

Since fear is so destructive, causing so much misery to its victims, why do people cling so tenaciously to their fears? Why not cast them gleefully aside and come alive in faith? Let me suggest some reasons...

(1) Those who fear do so because they are seeking protection. They trust their fear to keep them out of harm's way. Their fear is an instinct of self-preservation become malignant. But its very malignancy heightens the sense of urgent need to cling to fear, lest by its loss they become exposed to peril. They fear the loss of fear.

But what bitter and tragic irony this is! For it is fear above all that paralyses the soul, strips it of defence, and leaves it helpless before its foes!

(2) People cling to their fears because they possess a sense of unworthiness, which makes them feel that they deserve nothing good out of life. They are comfortable only in adversity. Prosperity fills them with alarm. If good things happen to them they feel guilty, as though they had stolen a joy that does not belong to them.

They have found that fear conveys to them a poverty of spirit, which they feel is their proper portion in this world; so fear seems to them to be a better servant than faith. The thought of releasing faith in God, of entering into a life of joyous abundance, of enjoying miracle upon miracle of answered prayer, of making melody every day, of deserving a superfluity of good things because they are children of God - all of that appalls them; it seems almost obscene, and certainly impious.

The God they worship afflicts them with leanness and the lash; any other concept of God is intolerable to them. They are seized by a kind of spiritual masochism that is a sad fusion of sincerity and carnal indulgence.

(3) A chief cause of people disguising their fears and giving them a pious garb, is a sense of guilt. They yearn to punish themselves for their sin. They do not want good things to happen to them, for this prevents them from obtaining religious satisfaction out of being punished for sin.

Like the self-flagellators of old, they measure their holiness by the degree of their sufferings. Without pain they cannot feel pure. Without sorrow they cannot feel saved. Without the rod they cannot feel righteous. Sadly, they never find the satisfaction they seek. Their guilt heightens their fear, their fear heightens their guilt, and their sufferings confirm both guilt and fear together.

Yet no price we can pay can ever ransom our souls or improve in the slightest the full atonement for sin offered by Christ on the cross. Only hideous pride, no matter how well that pride is disguised under pious sufferings, can allow any human being to think that God's perfect work of atonement can be bettered.

(4) Many people feel safe in their fears. They have lived so long in an environment of anxiety and inner trouble that any other way of life seems impossible. They are more comfortable with defeat than with victory; happier (or so they think) with poverty than with prosperity. They simply cannot hold to a mental image of themselves living joyfully in the Lord, strong, successful, vibrant, abundantly alive. That scene is somehow more threatening to them than the familiar one of their defeat.

But faith begins with a vision of the invisible, it is the evidence of things not seen. The things not seen must be seen, before faith can create a miracle. To faith the invisible is visible before it happens, and only then can it happen.

These people, however, because of their refusal to see anything beyond their present condition, are thwarted before they even begin. What they are, they are, and they cannot imagine any real change taking place.

Nor do they want to imagine anything else. Their greatest fear is of the unknown. They do not dare to think what life would be like if they were released from their bondage, if they were suddenly free to serve God in zestful liberty, or if they were faced with the challenge of handling an abundance of heavenly gifts. That "new man" in Christ is to them truly unimaginable.

These timorous souls really prefer their old familiar, fearful, defeated self. They have a slave mentality, doomed to wear chains, and they deserve the fetters they carry.

(5) Then there are those who use their fears as an excuse for clinging to things God has told them to surrender. Out of a fear of poverty, for example, they decline to give the money God has asked from them. Out of a fear of failure, or of personal weakness, they justify disobedience to God's command to attempt a great task for his glory.

> *"The Lord cannot blame me," they plead, "for he surely knows how timid I am, how slender my faith, how poor my resources."*

Fear becomes, to them, a justifiable reason for keeping well back from the front line of battle; it explains their failure to do what God has told them to do, or to be what he has commanded them to be.

For such reasons, and perhaps others as well, people cling to their fears.

But the scriptures allow no exceptions.

No matter who you are, no matter what your circumstances, the demand is emphatic, **"Fear not! Believe only!"** There is no possible evasion, no justifiable excuse. Those who come to God **must** believe, and the inescapable precursor to faith is to be rid of fear.

This theme will be taken up again in the next chapter, along with some powerful keys to living victoriously in Christ.

CHAPTER THREE

YOUR WORD OF FAITH

The previous chapter explored the problem of **fear** and how it paralyses faith. Perhaps the most graphic example of that chapter is found in the story of Jesus hushing the storm....

THERE IS NEVER ANY EXCUSE FOR FEAR

Please read Mt 8:23-27; Mk 4:35-41, and notice these statements -

"He said to them, `Why are you afraid, **you men of little faith**?'"

And again: "He said to them, `Why are you afraid? **Have you no faith**?'"

When you consider the circumstances in which Christ asked those questions, it is difficult not to think that he was being quite unreasonable. If ever a group of men had a right to be afraid, those men did on that stormy night! The gospels give a vivid description of the desperate peril they were facing -

> *"There arose a great storm on the sea, so that the boat was being swamped by the waves..."*
>
> *"And a great storm of wind arose, and the waves beat into the boat, so that the boat was already filling..."*

Their position was hopeless. They were already as dead men. There is no-one alive who would not have reacted as they did. They cried out, "Save us Lord; we are perishing! Don't you care that we are about to die!"

But I have misled you. There was one man alive who did not react with despair. Jesus. He was calmly sleeping on a cushion in the stern of the boat.

When the disciples in their terror awoke him, expecting to die with him, he calmed the storm. But then he made that astonishing demand: **"Why are you afraid?"**

Had I been there I am sure that a hundred good reasons for being desperately afraid would have sprung onto my lips: "Why am I afraid, Lord? Didn't you hear the wind screaming like a demon from hell? Can't you see how the boat is still wallowing, half-filled with water, and even now threatening to sink? Who could ever have dreamed that with a couple of words you could hush such a savage storm? Lord, my friends and I had every reason to be afraid. Any normal person would have been terrified!"

The disciples, it seems, had better sense than I; they said nothing. They simply accepted the Lord's rebuke, and went on to marvel at his authority over the wind and the sea. Perhaps they were so over-awed by the miracle that they hardly heard his rebuke.

But, I must admit, I find that **rebuke** - "Why are you afraid?" - more startling than the miracle of calming the storm. If Christ could ask that question of those imperilled men, then there is no conceivable circumstance in which fear is permissible. If Christ did not allow that those men had any reason to be afraid, then he will not allow anyone an excuse for fear.

There is no circumstance you can face more perilous than that terrifying night on Galilee; if fear was inexcusable then, it must always be inexcusable.[5]

Plainly, Christ reckoned that those men had no good reason to be afraid. Their fear was actually unreasonable. The cause of their fear was not the storm, nor the howling wind, nor even the raging sea; neither was it the water cascading into their boat. **The real cause of their fear was that they had discarded their faith**.

---

[5] Except of course a wise fear of God, and a sensible and positive instinct of self-preservation.

Yet God was still with them; the promise of God had not changed. So the sound of their voices should have been a shout of faith, not a cry of fear. They were "looking out" instead of "looking up"!

That is why the Lord demanded, "Where is your faith?"

After all, on the same lake, in the same storm, at the same hour, while the disciples in **fear** were stricken with panic, Christ in **faith** was sound asleep!

When he awoke, his mastery remained unchanged. With three calm words, "Peace, be still!" he brought the situation under control. But then, most amazing of all, he made it clear to his disciples that **they should have been able to do the same!** Had they known what it meant to fear not and believe only, their personal victory would have been as great as his.

How implacable is this demand for faith! How insistent the command to expose and banish every fear! The truth is irrevocable: **without faith it is impossible to please God.** And this story shows us two of the major factors in faith: mastery over fear; and authority expressed by a spoken command.

Those two powerful ideas are explored in the next section....

YOUR WORD OF FAITH AND AUTHORITY

In life's storms there are three things you can do....

>	go under in fear . . . collapsing without God.

>	go at it fighting . . . calling on God.

>	go over in faith . . . conquering with God!

We see those three approaches exemplified in Moses and Israel[6]...

With mighty signs and wonders Moses had brought the people of Israel out of Egypt (Ex 12:35-36), resplendent with the health and

---

[6] This section is based on a pamphlet of mine, by the same title, which has had a circulation of many thousands.

glory of God. There was not one sick or feeble person among them! (Ps 105:37-43).

But then they came to that crisis by the Red Sea. See their reactions! They were three-fold. Three voices could be plainly heard -

> there was the voice of the people, a voice of **fear** - defeated;

> then above the clamouring crowd Moses spoke out, and his was the voice of **hope** - waiting;

> but then God revealed himself; and he spoke the word of **faith** - triumphant!

The people saw the Red Sea, the desert, the Egyptian army - and in a flood of despair they collapsed. Before the battle was ever joined they were defeated by their fear.

Moses, too, saw the threatening grey waves and the searing desert. He watched the dust haze of the approaching chariots and soldiers. He took stock of all this, then remembered the might and mercy of God, and uttered those words of encouragement and prayer that have unfortunately been admired by countless people across the ages:

> *"Fear not! Stand still! See the salvation of the Lord, which he will show to you today!" (Ex 14:13-14)*

Perhaps you are protesting: "What do you mean, those words have been **unfortunately** admired? Surely they are a great example of brave trust in God? Surely God was pleased with them?"

No, God was **not** pleased, as you will discover if you read on -

Asking and Acting

Moses' words did not ring true. In fact, despite their show of courage and faith, **God condemned him for them**. Why? Because when Moses said, "Stand still," he revealed a profound spiritual weakness. That was the cry, not of faith, but of a defeated man!

Like the people he was leading, Moses had seen the danger of the hour and had concluded that this was beyond their resources. With the voice of hope he commanded the people to stand still and wait, to face the danger, to fight it out, trusting that God would deliver them.

No doubt there was some truth in that hopeful cry. But had Israel followed Moses' advice, a fierce and bitter battle must have followed, and thousands of God's people would have been slaughtered.

Then God spoke: **"Why are you crying out to me?"**

The Lord rebuked Moses for **praying** when he should have been **doing**. There is a time to **ask** but also a time to **act**. There is a time to seek **from** the Lord, but also a time to speak **for** the Lord!

So God commanded Moses to speak to the people, to strike the waters with his rod and to go across in victory.

That was the voice of **faith**, commanding and conquering.

The Red Sea And Your Rod Of Authority

What is the "Red Sea" in your life?

Have you reached a place where there seems to be no hope, and you feel shut in on every side? Do all your past victories seem far away, while a host of howling "Egyptians" is relentlessly bearing down on you? Are you chained and bound by some Satanic oppression - perhaps a dominating sin, or a ruinous disease? Perhaps some crippling habit, or some inner weakness that drives you again and again into failure? Has disaster shattered your hopes, destroyed your dreams, brought you to despair?

In the face of these things, what are you doing?

Some people throw their faith to the four winds. The bitter cry of their heart is "curse God and die!"

Others stand and fight. With great courage and pure trust they grapple with the darkness and wrestle through the long night, standing, hoping, praying, waiting for the salvation of God. Many times this comes, but oh! with what loss. Some fight the battle too hard. Becoming embittered, they finally surrender to the forces of evil.

But God wants you to face your "Red Sea" boldly and, triumphantly shouting "I am more than a conqueror through Christ," to strike the troubled waters with the rod of faith, and march forward.

Your Powerful Word of Faith

The rod Moses held was the emblem of divine authority. It was given by God as an outward sign that all the power of heaven stood behind him as he spoke in the name of the Lord.

To us, it is symbolic of the Word of God and the believer's authority in Christ.

Now, many Christians do not know that they have any authority. But see what the Bible says....

> *I have given you authority over all the power of the enemy" (Lu 10:19)*

On the cross the Lord Jesus Christ "spoiled principalities and powers, and made an open show of them, and triumphed over them." To every believer is given the right to share in this glorious conquest. Having gained absolute command over Satan and his evil hordes, Christ has now fully conferred this victory and dominion upon his disciples. We must open our eyes to see that we can, by faith, easily crush underfoot every wile and work of Satan, and even the arch-fiend himself!

The authority over the devil that we possess in Christ goes far beyond that which Moses exercised before Pharaoh, and infinitely exceeds all the resources Satan can muster. The powers of evil are compelled to obey you as you stand in the name of Jesus and exert your faith and authority against them.

Those principalities and potentates of iniquity may resist you; perhaps by cunning wiles they will endeavour to turn you aside from your steadfast stand; they may hurl against you all their hatred and malignity; **but nevertheless, they must finally yield before the authority of your faith.**

So long as you stand beneath the precious blood of Jesus, refusing to allow the enemy to bring any accusation against you, but holding against him the incomparable name of Jesus, you will prevail, and he will flee in abject defeat. "We overcome Satan by the blood of the Lamb and by the word of our testimony" (Re 12:11).

"If God is for us who can be against us?" (Ro 8:31)

It might seem that the whole world is against you. But they cannot succeed in their opposition so long as you know by faith that God is on **your** side and that you cannot fail.

"We are more than conquerors!" (Ro 8:37)

The apostle has to resort to repeated superlatives in an effort to depict the immense victory we have in Christ. He is not satisfied with affirming that Christ has made us conquerors; rather, he thrusts into an astonishing new realm of victory by declaring that we are **more than** conquerors!

Satan will certainly try to entice you from this place of sovereignty. He will endeavour to burden you with confusion or guilt. He will attack you with fretfulness or depression. He will try to push you beyond a proper sorrow for sin into a wallow of endless denigration. He will try to turn your eyes onto yourself and your weakness, and away from God and his infinite might. He will try to centre your "affections on things on earth" rather than on "those things which are above, where Christ sits at the right hand of God" Col 3:1-3). Rather than allow you to believe that "you are risen with Christ", he will try to convince you that you are irretrievably fallen into ruin.

But so long as you have confessed your sin, you must resolutely believe that by the blood of Jesus you are brought far above Satan's accusations, and that you are now enthroned in the heavenlies in perfect union with Christ (Ep 2:4-6).

Though you were "dead in sin", yet now "God has quickened you together with Christ" and raised you up with him into the place of grace and glory. Claim the protection and strength of the Holy Spirit; rest beneath the covering shroud of the covenant; vigorously resist the enemy, and unhesitatingly demand your rights against him!

> *"But thanks be to God, who in Christ always leads us in triumph!"... "God is able to make all grace abound to you, so that in all things at all times, having all that you need, you will abound in every good work." (2 Co 2:14; 9:8).*

If God's work is to be done in our day, and the church is to stand victorious in this hour, it is surely essential for every Christian to learn how to maintain constant victory in Christ.

In a furious, desperate effort, Satan is marshalling all his powers for a terrible assault on the church. It is urgent that we now accept, and rejoice in, the provision made for us in Christ of total spiritual authority. We must rise with fearless faith in God, take our seat with Christ in the heavenly realm, and hold the enemy and all his works under complete subjection to our word of command!

> *"Be strong in the Lord and in the power of his might" (Ep 6:10; 1:19-20; 3:20).*

The Lord Jesus Christ is absolute head over all principality, power, might, and dominion, and over every name that is named, both in this world and in the world to come. His control and his government are supreme. Risen from the grave and seated now at the right hand of the Majesty on high, he rules far above every other force or being in the entire universe.

The folly of Satan is exposed in his futile rebellion against our sovereign Lord. As though an autumn leaf were to declare war upon the cold wind, or an ephemeral mist to challenge a mighty hurricane. How absurd! God has spoken: the supremacy of Christ, and of those who take their place beside him in faith, is unshakeable; his, and their, right to rule can never be disputed.

By the grace of God, through the exceeding riches of his kindness toward us, we have been elevated into the honour of Christ. By faith we become identified with Christ; what Christ is, we see ourselves to be; we reckon ourselves to be strong with his strength; our power is found in his might. Mark these words -

> *"How tremendous is the power available to us who believe in God. That power is the same divine energy that was demonstrated in Christ when he raised him from the dead and gave him the place of supreme honour in heaven - a place that is infinitely superior to any conceivable command, authority, power, or control ... (and) now ... by his power within us (he) is able to do infinitely more than we ever dare ask or imagine" (Ep 1:19-20; 3:20; Phillips).*

"I can do all things in him who strengthens me. Strengthened with all power, according to his glorious might" *(Ph 4:13; Col 1:11).*

In the light of such scriptures how could you ever give place to the devil? How could you ever yield to the feeble forces of your ancient foe when the measure of your God-given strength is "according to his glorious power"?

How do you know when Satan is attacking you and when to arm yourselves with the armour and might of God (Ep 6:10-18)?

Here are the signs of Satan's depredations: anything that hinders or destroys your attitude of worship, peace, love, and joy in the Holy Spirit; whatever removes or clouds your consciousness of the presence of God; inward accusation and condemnation, especially if it continues after sin has been confessed and placed beneath the blood; temptation to sin, for "God tempts no man with sin"; dissension in home or church; virulent diseases - all these are the marks of Satan. Such things show that our "adversary, the devil, is (still) going about like a roaring lion, seeking whom he may devour."

Satan will not let go unless you compel him to; he will not relinquish his usurped authority, unless you boldly and aggressively challenge him with your legal rights in Christ and force him to give place before you.

But you **can** resist him, for the strength of God is put in your hand as you take hold of God's Word, and the authority of God is put in your mouth as you joyfully speak that word in the name of Jesus.

If Satan still grips you, do not despair or rail against God. Rather, stir up your **faith**, for that is the key to victory. The promise is sure: by his death Christ has rendered the devil powerless - unless by unbelief you strip Christ of his victory and give back to Satan his old rights against you. But only stand in obedient faith, opposing the devil in every place where you find his work, and you will soon discover how complete was the rout Jesus inflicted on the kingdom of darkness at the cross, and how overwhelming is the promise of triumph that he has now conferred on you!

> *"Christ in you, the hope of glory" (Col 1:27).*

May God enable us who believe in Christ to arise from the spiritual lethargy into which the delusions of Satan have thrust us. May we awake from the false weakness that we have induced by describing ourselves as still fallen, still separated from God by sin, still without strength, still void of spiritual power.

Christians often feel that they are hemmed in by foes and forces that are mightier than they; yet scripture says that all of the infinite majesty of heaven is within our grasp! We must learn to stop judging by appearances, to refrain from depending only on what we can see and feel with the natural senses.

Notice that your natural senses can bring you evidence only of things that are transitory, temporary, and, comparatively unreal! That is because this earth, and the fashion of it, is doomed to pass away.

But the things that are in heaven, the things that faith alone can discern, are eternal. **True reality is found only in God.** He alone is the one great Author of all. The earth and all it contains, and the vast universe beyond, exist only so long as God permits. We must cultivate the spiritual art of seeing the invisible. Our trust should be, not in those visible things that the natural senses so readily discern, which soon perish, but rather in the unassailable reality of God's spiritual promise. The apostles understood this secret, hence their mighty power - "By faith they endured, because they **saw** him who is **invisible!**" (He 11:27).

What can make the invisible visible? Only faith!

There is a vision in faith that enables you to see the Christ who is in you - and if you have **Christ** what more do you need? If you have Christ, you have **glory**, the glory of God, and all that this glory contains of abundant life, health, and constant victory.

Jesus said, "Believe, and you will see the glory of God!" The world says, "Seeing is believing". But God says, **"Believing is seeing!"**

God's word is truth, and that word declares that Christ is in you. Do not listen then to the devil's lies, whispering that you are weak, that you have no faith, that your love is cold, and so on. If you have Christ in you, and believe it, and if you live in the consciousness of his indwelling presence, you cannot help but have all those things that you need to triumph always, and day by day to show the glory of God!

> *"You are complete in him!" (Col 2:10).*

If Christ is in you what more can you want? What more can God give you? If you have Christ you have all! You are **complete**! Nothing more that is necessary to you can be given.

Even the day of his coming will effect no essential change. Certainly you will then be loosed from the old mortal body of clay, and you will be changed; but this change will only involve a revelation of that resurrection body and glory which is already planted in you (see Col 3:4; 1 Co 15:42-44; Ro 8:30; Jn 17:22).

On that day the glory **which is in you now** will be manifested for all to see. You will believe it then, no doubt, and will have no trouble in treading Satan underfoot. You will believe it then, because your eyes will see it. But why not believe it now, because God's Word declares it? You will have no more authority then than is given you now, no more glory then than belongs to you now, no more of Christ then than you have now. It will only become more apparent.

In the coming age, of course, Satan will be bound once and for all, and we will all be removed forever from the corruptions and temptations of this world. Those will be great privileges, gifts of inestimable value - especially the priceless joy of seeing Jesus face to face. We wait with impatient gladness for the stunning arrival of the visible kingdom of God. Yet that does not alter the fact that the fundamental reality of all of those treasures belongs to you right now.

Already Christ is in you. Already you can "with open face behold as in a mirror the glory of the Lord, and be changed into the same image from glory to glory! (2 Co 3:18) Already it is true that you are complete in Christ and have no need of any other gift, for in Christ you have all. Already you may affirm that you are dead indeed to sin and alive to God! (Ro 6:11). Right now you have a God-given authority over Satan and all the kingdom of darkness, and you may grind that serpent the devil underfoot. **Today**, not tomorrow, you have a God-given right to believe, and believing, to rejoice with joy unspeakable and full of glory (1 Pe 1:8).

So look into your heart and see Christ there, and yourself complete in him. Look up to heaven, and see yourself raised with Christ, seated with him on his throne, and reigning in the strength and dominion of your God. Speak no more of your lack, but only of your all-sufficiency in Christ.

Creating Your Own Miracle

Come back with me again to the Red Sea, and to the rod of authority that God gave to Moses.

Do you believe in the Lord Jesus Christ? Are you a child of God? Then you have an authority that far surpasses that of Moses! Your authority was gained for you by the mighty victory of Christ on the cross (Col 2:13-15; 3:1-4).

As a believer with heaven's authority committed to you, what you **say** to the "Red Sea" is more important than what you **pray** about it.

Moses discovered this powerful truth when God told him to stop standing there helplessly praying, and to **command** the waters to roll back.

Jesus taught the same lesson when he showed the disciples how to handle those mountains that rear themselves before us as we journey along - the mountains of sin, sickness, and suffering. The Lord said, "Whoever shall **say** to this mountain, `Be removed!'... shall have whatever he says!" (Mk 11:23) Mark this: you must "say" to the **mountain**, not "pray" to **God**! There is a time to ask and a time to act; a time to pray, but a time also to press forward in the commanding authority and conquering might of faith.

We are all wholly dependent on prayer, and we must be diligent to pray always. Jesus himself taught us that (Lu 18:1-8; etc.).

But nonetheless, when God speaks, as he did to Moses, and as he will do to you - perhaps through prayer, or by his written promise, or by the impulse of his Spirit - it is time then to rise up boldly and, like Gideon, to "go in this your might!" Then is the time to speak in faith, to command Satan to loose his hold, to command that mountain to be cast into the sea, to command that circumstance to change, and to watch faith overcome the world!

Almost above anything else, what you say shapes your life (Pr 6:2; Mt 12:37).

Many scriptures confirm that principle. Here are some of them -

Ro 10:9 - the words of faith that you speak seal your salvation.

He 3:1 - Christ is the high priest of your **confession**. The Greek word translated "confession" implies that you must say the same thing as God, and that Christ will then take the things that you say and present them to his Father, who will confirm them with his own mighty power (Mk 16:20). After the Lord told Moses to speak, Moses stopped **praying** and instead **spoke** with the authority of God. Only then did the Lord stretch out his hand and roll back the waters of the barricading ocean.

Ac 3:6 - With authority Peter **spoke to** the lame man, and he was healed by God's power, through the name of the Lord Jesus Christ. See also Ac 13:11; 16:18.

Ge 1; and He 11:3 - The Lord looked into the vast emptiness of space, and spoke! From nothing the worlds came into being. Mighty word!

Ro 4:17-21 - Do you realise that God says that things which don't exist, do exist? "He calls those things that **are not** as though they **are**" (lit.) Abraham recognised this, refused to consider his own age or his wife's, or the utter impossibility of a son being born to them, but with bold faith declared that God's promise was true, and that the impossible would be done.

Right now, with complete confidence, begin to affirm your victory in Christ; demand your rights; by faith strike the waters; speak to the darkness and compel the light to come. As with Moses, in a little while the wind of God will begin to blow, the power of the Holy Spirit will begin to change the face of the waters, and when you awake in the morning there will be a highway of deliverance right through the ocean!

> *Resist the devil and he will flee from you! (Ja 4:7; 1 Pe 5:7-11).*

Now this matter of the spoken word of faith is so important, and it has such exciting ramifications, it deserves a separate study. So the next chapter will take up this theme again, and you will discover in it amazing things about your own word of faith and authority!

CHAPTER FOUR

SPEAK THE WORD

"Just speak the word, and my servant will be healed!" (Mt 8:8).

When Jesus heard that saying from a Roman centurion he was astonished. He had not found any other person with such great faith. The centurion was the first person the Lord had met who had understood the real nature of faith. He was the first man (apart from Jesus) to express the key place occupied by the spoken word in the exercise of spiritual authority.

Jesus was indeed surprised; but it could not be denied. The Roman actually had grasped this great principle: **faith and spiritual authority are expressed through words.** The centurion had discovered that nothing can resist the spoken word of faith; that is, nothing can resist God's word, for nothing can be spoken by faith that does not have its origin in God.

So the Roman said to Jesus, **"Speak the word only!"**

He knew that just one command given in the authority of faith would rout sickness and bring life out of death. And so it happened. Jesus spoke. And in that same hour the centurion's servant was healed.

There are many scriptures that emphasise the importance and power of the words we speak, scriptures which show that we too can "speak a word only" and see miracles happen. In fact, since there are so many references it is astonishing that so few Christians have understood this principle or used it to tap the glorious resources of heaven.

In this lesson we are going to explore in greater detail **the power of your faith-confession** and to highlight some of the exciting things the Bible teaches about this great spiritual principle.

The plan I have followed is simply to take each major reference in order, and to support those primary texts with other lesser references. The ideas will therefore be discussed, not necessarily in logical order, nor in order of importance, but in scriptural order.

GOD'S METHOD IS TO SPEAK A WORD

What is the very first thing we are told about God in the Bible?

You might answer, "That he created the heavens and the earth, and all that is in them."

But that is not quite true. More accurately, we are told that he called the entire universe into being **simply by speaking** -

> *"God **spoke** ... and it was so" (Ge 1:1,3).*

> *"The world was created by the command of God, so that what is seen was made out of things that do not appear" (He 11:3).*

God's unchanging method has been to use a creative command. Whatever he does, is done simply by the awesome power of his word -

> *"But I the Lord will speak the word which I will speak, and it will be performed" (Ez 12:25).*

Not only was the universe created out of nothing by the spoken word of God, but that same powerful word still upholds the entire creation (He 1:3). If God should ever withdraw or countermand his word, the universe would vanish - which will in fact one day happen (He 1:10-12).

Now we need to grasp this fact: **God achieves all of his mighty works by a simple word of faith**. Knowledge of this is the one thing that can convey to us a sense of the enormous power vested in scripture, **which contains the words of God**, and through which we gain access to God's irresistible word.

Any person who comes into a proper relationship with scripture makes contact with the stupendous force that called the heavens and earth into being out of nothing! Any person who takes hold of the promises of the Bible, and boldly affirms them, is speaking the very words of God - and those words can have as much creative power on your lips as they do on God's.

God has such confidence in his word that he speaks into empty space and says that things which do not yet exist do exist! The non-existent is called into being solely by his word.

This divine law was the booster that launched Abraham's faith to such soaring heights (Ro 4:16-22). His faith conquered death, brought forth a marvellous miracle, and is still having a profound effect in millions of lives today!

Abraham had received a promise from God that tested his faith to the limit. God said that he would father a child in his old age. But he showed unswerving confidence in God's ability to keep the promise, so a miracle of answered prayer was granted to him and Sarah.

On what ground did Abraham build this great faith? We are told that he knew two things that made him absolutely certain God would never be embarrassed by an inability to keep his word: he knew firstly that God gives life to the dead; and secondly that God calls those things that do not exist as though they do exist (vs 17) ....

God Gives Life To The Dead

I don't know how Abraham came to know this about God - perhaps he had seen the Lord actually raise a person from the dead; or perhaps he just realised that there could be no imaginable limit to the power of him who created all that exists.

But I do know that my wife and I have good reason to share Abraham's faith, for we have two sons who are literally alive from the dead! According to medical science they should both have perished in their mother's womb. But we refused to surrender our little ones to the darkness. We respected the opinion of my wife's doctors; but we believed that God's word was higher and his ability greater! Each day my wife was pregnant I laid my hands on her in prayer and claimed the promise God had given us. Now my two grown sons, Eric and Baden, are abundant proof to us that God can keep his promise. **He gives life to the dead, and nothing is too hard for him!** (cp. Ge.18:13-14).

God Calls That Which Is Not As Though It Is
THE ULTIMATE POSSIBILITY

To say that "God calls those things that are not as though they are" is the ultimate way of saying that nothing is impossible for God. It could be argued that when it comes to raising the dead there is at least a corpse to begin with! There is something to work on! But the ultimate test of God's skill is to say to him, "Here is nothing, see what you can do with it!" And what can God do with nothing? Everything! And he needs only his word to do it!

Now, if you know those two things about God, then you will know that it is easy for God to keep his promise. What he has promised he is able to perform. The only hard thing God faces is to persuade us to believe as Abraham believed, and to speak the word of faith, God's word, as Abraham spoke it!

But if you can bring yourself to believe with Abraham that God gives life to the dead and that he calls those things that are not as though they are, then you too will become a recipient of the eternal power that created all that exists! If you, like Abraham, "do not waver concerning the promise of God, but grow strong in faith as you give glory to God, being fully convinced that God is able to do what he has promised" (vs 21), then you too will experience an exhilarating flow of divine life and power.

Nothing will be impossible to you!

You will speak God's word into the empty void of poverty, disease, failure, sin, fear, and call into existence miracles of divine deliverance and of abundant supply.

The Ultimate Test

According to the RSV, and other translations, my text reads, "(God) calls into existence the things that do not exist."

That is a true enough statement; but as a translation it is rather pedestrian. It lacks sparkle. The original Greek is far more punchy. In fact this is a classic example of one of those passages of scripture that commentators and translators block their minds against. They simply cannot come to terms with it. What it actually says is emotionally unacceptable to them. They are able neither to receive it nor to express it accurately in their own words. So they soften its impact. Not with any deliberate intent to misrepresent scripture, but simply because they cannot grasp what the passage actually says. They subconsciously refuse to accept it and so they modify the divine revelation.

May I hasten to say, I am not trying to imply here that I and I alone am true while the rest of the world is false! There may well be other passages of scripture where I have the same kind of mental block. It often takes a revelation of God to put real meaning into a passage of scripture (cp. Ep 1:15-18). Some of the ideas in scripture are just too breath-taking, too incredible, to be received until you are ready to receive them (cp. He 5:11-14; 1 Pe 1:10-12).

But I hope that you are ready to receive the idea I want to share with you now! So, back to the text ....

The Original Greek

In the original Greek it reads like this: "He (Abraham) believed God, the (one) calling the not being as being." Now that is an explicit statement: the God Abraham believed in is the one **who calls that which has no being as though it does have being.** But that is such an astonishing statement, almost akin to calling black white, or empty full, or death life, that translators back away from it, and dull its impact. Some examples -

> "God calls into existence things that do not exist" (RSV)
>
> "God speaks his word to those who are yet unborn" (Phillips)
>
> "God calls into being what does not exist" (Moffatt)

"God calls into being that which does not exist" (NASB)

"God calls into being what does not exist" (Jerusalem)

"God continually anticipates the birth of things that give as yet no token of existence" (Way)

"God calls into existence what has no being" (Berkeley)

"God calls into being even things that do not exist" (Barclay)

With the exception of J. B. Phillips, who paraphrases the text almost out of existence, all of those translators have attempted to be true to the scripture but also to express it in terms that are emotionally and logically acceptable. They come up with a rendering essentially identical in each case, and one that is true in what it says about God, for he does indeed call into existence things that do not exist.

Yet in the end those translators really do make the same error as Phillips: the error of reducing the text to a human level.

Notice that **"speaking a word to those who are as yet unborn"**, or **"calling into existence things that do not exist",** are not exclusively divine attributes. Many men and women have left sayings behind them that have spoken powerfully, and still speak, to succeeding generations. Any creative artist calls into existence something which did not previously exist.

Admittedly God can and does do both of those things to a vastly greater degree; but the difference is still one of degree, not kind.

The text, on the other hand, speaks about an attribute that **belongs uniquely to God** and to those who are his children in faith (as Abraham was).

What is that attribute? Read on ....

What The Text Really Says

Two translators come nearer to the real meaning of the text, although they still manage to avoid its stunning impact for today by relegating it to the future, that is, to fulfilled prophecy-

> *"God speaks of the non-existent things (that he has foretold and promised) as if they already existed" (ANT).*

> *"God speaks of future events with as much certainty as though they were already past" (Taylor).*

Those translations certainly express part of the inner meaning of the text, for they at least talk about something only God can do. But they are at still at fault, because they limit it to the single field of predicting the future.

But I did find on my shelves four translations bold enough to say exactly what the text says -

> *"God calleth those things which be not as though they were" (AV)*

> *"God calls those things that are not as though they were" (NIV)*

> *"God speaks of things non-existent as though existing" (Weymouth)*

> *"God summons things that are not yet in existence as though they already were" (NEB)*

Now we have come to the real heart of the matter. Here is that unique characteristic of divine faith I have already discussed with you: **faith is the evidence of things not seen, the substance of things hoped for.** Faith sees what is not there to be seen - except by faith! Faith grips tomorrow so hard it becomes today!

Thus faith copies God, for God looks at things that don't exist and says they do exist, and behold, they exist! God speaks into empty space, and says there is a universe, and it is there. He speaks into sin, says there is righteousness, and it is there. He speaks into sickness, says there is health, and it is there. He speaks into death, says there is life, and it is there. He speaks into poverty, says there is abundance, and it is there!

The Rule Of Faith

The rule is simply this: the only reality God recognises is his word.

What he says is, is; what he says is not, is not!

God does not bend his word to suit the circumstances, he compels the circumstances, indeed the entire universe, to conform to his word.

The word God speaks is irresistible, it destroys all other reality and creates a new reality, it conforms to nothing except itself.

Abraham recognised this principle, and aligned himself with it. He refused to consider his own "dead" body, or the deadness of Sarah's womb, and embraced instead the word God spoke to him. In front of the absolute truth of God's word he counted every other witness a liar. He spurned the lesser reality (his dead body), and seized the greater (the divine word).

Thus faith changed the impossible into the possible. Death became life, and Abraham brought into existence that which did not exist.

A Definition Of Faith

So now we can attempt another definition: faith recognises the absolute integrity and irresistible force of God's word, seeks to discover that word and then to pronounce it boldly, knowing that the word has the same creative power when spoken by man as it has when spoken by God.

Moses received a word from God: by it he smashed the power of imperial Egypt and set captive Israel free.

Joshua received a word from God: he drove back flooding Jordan, brought down the walls of Jericho, stayed the sun in its course across the sky, and conquered the promised land.

David received a word from God: he slew the lion and the bear, cut off Goliath's head, and was raised to the throne of Israel.

Elijah received a word from God: he was fed by ravens, gave the widow a supernatural supply of oil and meal, raised the dead boy to life, called down fire from heaven, and turned a nation back to God.

Elisha received a word from God: he divided the waters of Jordan, turned poison into sweet food, made iron swim, raised the dead, healed the sick, and called down the vengeance of God upon unbelievers.

Isaiah received a word from God: he healed the dying king, and compelled the shadow to retreat ten degrees.

So likewise did many other heroes of faith, in the days of old Israel.

But then the servants of God in the church did the same. Inspired by the example of Christ himself the apostles and disciples walked on water, overcame poison, healed the sick, walked out of barred prisons, raised the dead, and performed many mighty signs, wonders, and miracles. Many of them too, in the strength of that same word, surrendered themselves to nakedness, hunger, shipwreck, wild beasts, tortures, and even death, knowing that the splendour of the resurrection was already theirs.

But all of them knew this law: faith calls those things that do not exist as though they do exist.

Faith looks into sin and summons righteousness to itself as though it already existed. Faith looks into sickness and summons health to itself as though it already existed. Faith looks into poverty and failure and summons prosperous success to itself as though they already existed.

Indeed, faith behaves the same way in the presence of **anything** that is contrary to God's will, or that seeks to exist in opposition to God's word.

Faith allows existence to nothing except what the word God has spoken allows.

An awesome and profound example of the value God attaches to his word was given when God made it the most magnificent title borne by his own Son - "The Word" (Jn 1:1-3).

The psalmist, too, caught a vision of this mighty secret when he sang with joy: "Thou hast exalted thy word above all thy name!" (Ps 138:2).

"Thy word" there means more than just a printed book. It means rather "THE WORD", Christ himself. But of course there is a marvellous union between Christ, the Living Word, and the Bible, the Written Word.

Just as a man's spoken words reflect his personality and nature, his meanness or his greatness, so Christ, *"reflects the glory of God and bears the very stamp of God's nature"* (He 1:3). The same Bible that says God created the heavens and the earth by the words he spoke, also says he created all things by Christ (Col 1:15-16). All that is held together by the word of God is also held together by Christ (vs 17).

Hence that incredible saying quoted above: *"God has magnified his word above all his name."* How great is the name of God, how magnificent, and how much to be revered! But his word stands higher, more to be praised, more to be admired, alongside God himself, for God and his word are one, as God and Christ are one, for Christ and the Word are one.

To reject the word of God, then, is to reject Christ, and to reject Christ is to reject the word of God. God attaches great importance to his word! All of the immeasurable strength of the Deity lies behind that word!

Our task then is two-fold: (1) to believe all that God speaks to us; and then, having heard God speak, (2) boldly to speak that word ourselves, and so call into existence the answer to our prayers.

MOSES WAS TAUGHT THE SAME LESSON

Please read Nu 20:1-13.

Moses learned the hard way! The penalty for his failure to depend only on the spoken word was exclusion from the Holy Land. He saw it from a distance, but never set foot on it. He lost everything, because he went beyond **speaking**. He did not believe that the spoken word was enough.

Many people are still being excluded from the promised land because they have not learned to speak the word of faith.

God told Moses to assemble the people and he said to Moses: **"Tell** the rock before their eyes to yield its water; thus **you** will bring water out of the rock for them, and **you** will give drink to the congregation and their cattle."

That was God's word to Moses. It was a divine promise. All that Moses had to do was to take the promise, act on it, and speak it into being. Simply by speaking to the unyielding rock he would cause it to yield water - rivers of water - enough and more for all the people.

Thus by **speaking in faith** he was to emulate the divine pattern and call into existence that which did not exist. Sadly, he failed, and bore a heavy punishment. In mercy, God still caused the water to flow abundantly, and the people were satisfied; but a principle of faith had been violated and a penalty had to be exacted.

Many people are puzzled by this incident, because on an earlier occasion Moses had in fact been told to strike a rock, not merely to **speak** to it (Ex 17:1-7).

Perhaps a solution to the mystery can be found in Paul's comparison of those two rocks with Christ:

> *"(They) all drank the same supernatural drink, for they drank from the supernatural Rock which followed them, and the Rock was Christ"* (1 Co 10:4).

Notice that Paul joins the two rocks together in his simile, and makes them one Rock, a picture of Christ. Now the first rock, by the command of God, had to be **struck** before it would yield its refreshing streams; but the second rock had only to be **told** to do so.

It has been suggested that here is a picture of the once – for - all sufferings of Christ. He has once been struck and wounded at Calvary, but he can be struck no more. Now he invites his friends just to **speak the word**, to command him concerning all that he has promised, and in the faith of God to tell every mountain to be laid low and every valley to be filled.

In the words of the old version, it is the same invitation God gave through the prophet:

> *"Thus saith the Lord, the Holy One of Israel, and his Maker. Ask me of things to come concerning my sons, and concerning the work of my hands* **command ye me!**" *(Is 45:11, AV).*

Ask God what his purpose is for you; ask him what he desires you to have; and when you have received a word from him, then boldly command that word to be fulfilled. Speak what God has spoken to you and it will come to pass!

Now let Job add a supporting comment (also in the words of the old version):

> *"How forcible are right words! ...* **Thou shalt decree a thing, and it shall be established unto thee**: *and the light shall shine upon thy ways"* *(6:25; 22:27-28).*

WHEN YOU BELIEVE, SPEAK!

"I believed, therefore have I spoken." So said the psalmist, and he encapsuled this great rule of faith we are now discussing. If you believe it, **speak it!** Your speaking will turn belief into a reality (Ps 116:10. AV).

Paul endorsed this. He quoted the psalm: "Since we have the same spirit of faith as he had who wrote, `I believed, and so I spoke'; **we too believe, and so we speak**, knowing that he who raised the Lord Jesus will raise us also with Jesus and bring us with you into his presence" (2 Co 4:13-14).

If you have the same spirit of faith as the psalmist and the apostle, then you too will not be content merely to **believe** the word; like them, you will be constrained also to **speak** it.

What is the measure of the power the spoken word can release?

Paul tells us.

It is equivalent to the mighty power God exercised when he raised Jesus from the dead. It is the same power he will exercise when Christ returns and our mortal bodies are raised incorruptible and beautiful, bearing his indescribable loveliness!

There is no need you can face in this life for which this power is not adequate! If you can believe it and speak it, you will have it!

DEATH AND LIFE ARE IN YOUR TONGUE

The book of Proverbs has much to say about the power of the tongue. Here are some of the more important references -

> *"From the fruit of his words a man is satisfied with good" (12:14).*
>
> *"He who guards his mouth preserves his life; he who opens wide his lips comes to ruin" (13:3).*
>
> *"To make an apt answer is a joy to a man, and a word in season, how good it is!" (15:23).*
>
> *"Pleasant words are like a honeycomb, sweetness to the soul and health to the body" (16:24).*
>
> *"The words of a man's mouth are deep waters" (18:4)*
>
> *"From the fruit of his mouth a man is satisfied; he is satisfied by the yield of his lips. Death and life are in the power of the tongue, and those who love it will eat its fruits" (18:20-21).*
>
> *"He who keeps his mouth and his tongue keeps himself out of trouble." (21:23).*

> *"A word fitly spoken is like apples of gold in a setting of silver" (25:11).*
>
> *"Do you see a man who is hasty in his words? There is more hope for a fool than for him" (29:20).*

No doubt most of those references are intended simply to contrast the ruin that overtakes those who speak carelessly or destructively with the benefits of discreet conversation. And it is certainly true that courteous and pleasant speech will bring much gain to any person, whereas sorrow is bound to overtake those whose speech is ill-considered or malicious.

But there is a still deeper meaning to be observed; for what is true of daily human conversation is even more true in the realm of the spirit. Speak good words of faith, and you will be satisfied with the good fruit your words will create.

Guard your mouth, so that it speaks only in harmony with the heart of God, and you will surely preserve your life; but open your mouth wide to speak abusively, negatively, or sinfully, and spiritual ruin will swiftly fall upon you.

How good you will find it to speak the right word, in the right way, at the right time. You will find a joy in those pleasant words like the sweetness of honeycomb! It is indeed true that by your words you may bring disease to your flesh and heaviness to your spirit; but equally true that words of faith will bring God's own health to both your soul and your body. Make no mistake about it: keep your mouth under discipline, and you will keep yourself out of trouble; but yield yourself continually to hasty speech and you will share the indictment of fools.

This profound influence that the words we speak have upon our lives is stressed in two of the references given just above (Pr 18:4, 20, 21).

The first of them says: **"The words of a man's mouth are deep waters"**.

There is a vast mystery in our ability to express ourselves with words. The faculty of speech God has given us is a unique part of the divine image in man. Notice that the first thing we are told about God in scripture is that he **speaks**; the first thing we observe God doing is **speaking**; the first thing to **result** from God's spoken word was a mighty act of **creation**.

But after revealing God as primarily **the One who creates by speaking**, the Bible then says that God made man in his own divine likeness. And the first thing the man is described as doing is - **speaking**! (Ge 2:19-20).

Do you see the surprising connection? God gave to Adam the faculty of speech, and this was a direct expression of the image of God possessed by man. Furthermore, this vocal ability was not merely a means of basic communication, like the bark of a dog, or the song of a bird; rather, man, like God, was to speak with imagination and creativity. So Adam's first vocal act was the extraordinary feat of ascribing apt and accurate names "to all cattle, and to the birds of the air, and to every beast of the field."

In the context of scripture, the idea of Adam naming every creature involves much more than a mere biological classification. The Hebrews thought of names as having power to shape the inner nature and identity of those that bore them. So in a mysterious sense, Adam, by naming the animals, was becoming a partner with God in creation - his names were affecting the form and behaviour of each creature.

This profound ability that man has to conceive ideas that none except God has ever conceived before; this ability to compose a new song, to write a new poem, to produce a new novel, to create a new philosophy; this ability to change things, to create, to destroy, simply by speaking, appears to be uniquely human. It would seem that not even the holy angels possess such attributes of imagination and creativity.

In the whole creation it would seem that **God has shared his creative word only with man**. Out of this creative word all human achievement ultimately arises; without it, we would truly be naked apes.

Furthermore, it was originally God's intention that the human voice should possess not only **creative** power but also **controlling** power. God told man to go out and to "subdue" the earth, and to have "dominion" over all it contained (Ge 1:28-30). How was this control to be exercised? Not by "sweat" and "toil", for that kind of laborious dominion arose out of God's judgment on man's fallen state (Ge 3:17-19). But if not by mechanical contrivance and by his own effort, then the only method of control remaining to man is that used by God: **the authority of the spoken word**. Simply by speaking in the name of God, Adam and Eve were able to govern their world and so fulfil the purpose of God.

That kind of original dominion was almost entirely destroyed by sin; but it has been restored in a measure to all who have been brought into "the new creation" that God has now created in Christ. To us who believe, the voice of faith has been given again, and by that voice we can accomplish every good work the Father commands us to do.[7]

YOUR WORDS CONDEMN YOU OR JUSTIFY YOU

> *"I tell you, on the day of judgment men will render account for every careless word they utter; for by your words you will be justified, and by your words you will be condemned" (Mt 12:36-37).*

---

[7] I am not saying that Adam and Eve had no work to do with their hands. They were after all put into the Garden of Eden "to till it and keep it" (Ge. 2:15); but their work was to be a pleasurable and creative expression of faith, not a substitute for it. The spoken word of authority was to put a divine dynamic into the work of their hands. We too must employ every skill and strength God has given us; but we too are called to add divine resources to all that we do by the right use of the spoken word of faith.

That passage of scripture is commonly understood in a way that really makes nonsense of it. A picture is drawn of God, the Awful Judge, switching on a kind of celestial tape recorder, and replaying every wrong word the sinner has ever uttered. As the tally slowly mounts, the dread sentence is made more and more severe, while the sinner sinks to the ground crushed and broken. That is a caricature of what Jesus meant.

But consider another scenario....

The Words We Speak Have An Accumulative Effect

In the molding of character, hardly anything is more important than the words you speak. Your daily conversation irresistibly shapes the kind of person you are now, and the kind of person you will be seen to be at the throne of judgment.

A positive confession, harmonious with scripture, consonant with the Christ who indwells you, seasoned with grace, patient within the goodness of God, will build a character in you of holiness and victory.

By contrast, speech that is negative, ungodly, fearful, saturated with unbelief, will create a character consonant with itself, destined for ruin and the wrath of God.

It might be objected that I have reversed the true order by saying that character is determined by speech. Should it not be said that speech is determined by character? Which is true: that a man's walk is fixed by his talk; or his talk is fixed by his walk?

The fact is, there is a tough connection between both ideas. Conversation and conduct profoundly influence each other. As a man is, so will he speak; as he speaks, so will he be.

Initially, of course, the things that I spoke arose out of the kind of person I was - my character formed my speech. But as I became more articulate, and able to make an ever wider choice in the things I said, my daily words exercised an ever increasing influence on the formation of my character.

The grace of God in Christ is a marvellous gift to us here. For we know that we have become "a new creation in Christ, old things have passed away, and behold, all things have become new!" (2 Co 5:17). Christ has given us a new beginning, having made each one of us a new person, with a fresh opportunity to form a new pattern of speech and to create a new life-style.

Through Christ, the cruel nexus between your old sinful character and its negative and destructive style of speech has been broken, and you are now set free to speak in harmony with the word of God and so to establish within yourself a character that more and more reflects the image of Christ.

This inexorable effect of conversation on character will be inevitably exposed in the day of resurrection, at the judgment seat of Christ. The Judge will not have to recount your words one by one. Your true character will at once be apparent to every spectator; the full effect of the way you have spoken each day will be seen by all.

This is the sense, then, in which we shall have to give account in the day of judgment for the words that we speak: day by day, the things we say, and the way we say them, have an accumulative effect. They are shaping and molding us, building us into the kind of person each one will be shown to be on that day.

The actual words we have spoken will not have to be remembered; the effect they had on us the character they created, will be sufficient to show whether you and I deserve condemnation or commendation.

Your Unguarded Words Are The True Criterion of Character

Notice that Jesus said we shall all have account for every **careless** word we utter. "Careless" does not mean "evil". The Greek word is "*argos*", and it means unemployed, unprofitable; and by extension, thoughtless or unguarded. In our present context "*argos*" may be said to describe two kinds of speech -

(1) It is the speech of a person who makes no attempt to guard or discipline his tongue, who says whatever comes into his head, who

blurts out the first thing that enters his mind, who gives no thought to whether or not his words are gracious or vicious, helpful or destructive, godly or ungodly, wise or foolish.

"*Argos*" is actually made up of two words, which together mean "not working" - that is, inactive, lazy, careless.

And that is exactly the position of the person referred to here. This person will not work at governing his tongue. He reserves the right to say whatever he wants to say, without restraint; he speaks by impulse alone, he is controlled by his emotions. He is perfectly described in Ja 3:1-12, and he will reap the sorrowful harvest predicted there.

(2) It is the speech of all of us when we are not making a special effort to impress someone; that is, the things we say **when we are not watching our words.**

The idea is this: your **real character** is revealed not so much by the fine and carefully chosen words you speak when you are being careful to say just the right thing, but rather by the flow of daily conversation, the way you express yourself when you are not making a conscious effort to impress anyone.

Anyone will speak piously in church, or courteously to his employer, or pleasantly to his spouse when guests are present! But how do you speak when church is over, or when the boss is absent, or when the guests have gone? How does your conversation appear when it is no longer dressed up, but is wearing its working clothes?

You will not be measured by what you were in your "Sunday best", but by what you were in daily life. On the day of judgment, God will deal with your true character; and that, said Christ, is revealed by your "careless" words - that is, by the shape of your speech when you are **not** taking special care. That "careless" speech reveals what kind of person you really are at heart.

So there are two contrasting ideas here.

On the one hand, we must discipline and govern our tongues, for we cannot allow them free rein to say whatever they like whenever they like. To permit such loose conversation will certainly incur divine rebuke.

But on the other hand, we expect this disciplined speech to shape within us a better character, so that, without conscious effort, we shall naturally say the right things in the right way. Thus the end result of a guarded tongue is a diminishing need to exercise such care. Our "careless" words will then be as righteous as our "careful" words!

A Promise Or A Threat?

There is a tendency in many Christians to imagine that the phrase "careless words" refers only to sinful words; or, even worse, that Christ was condemning merely casual or humorous conversation.

But from what I have said, it should be obvious that these "careless" or "idle" words may just as readily be virtuous as wicked. Depending upon its nature, "careless" speech can be either proper or improper, life-giving or life-destroying, a source of salvation or of judgment, of justification or of condemnation (vs 37).

So the purpose of this passage of scripture is not to crush us with an intolerable burden, but to encourage us to be so open to the Holy Spirit that "the tree" of our lives will be "made good, and its fruit good" (vs 33).

We cannot change ourselves. If we are left to our own devices the indictment must fall upon us all: "You brood of vipers! how can you speak good, when you are evil!" (vs 34). We are bound to reply, "Your accusation is true, Lord; by ourselves we cannot possibly speak good!"

Yet our case is not hopeless, for in Christ we **can** discard that "old man" with his carnal conversation, and re-clothe ourselves with the "new man", which is made in God's image (Ep 4:22-25; Col 3:8-13).

It is a matter of choice and of reciprocal action.

We choose to act in faith, to cast off our old nature (because Christ has freed us from its fetters), and to put on our new nature. Then "out of the abundance" of this new heart our lips will certainly speak good (vs 34, 35). But then, as our lips speak good, the new nature will be built ever more firmly into us, which produces still more Christ-like speech.... and so a spiral of godliness is created as character and conversation continually interact upon each other.

"The tree is known by its fruit," said Jesus. Your speech will show your character, and your character will shape your speech. It is the amalgamation of these things, and the end result they produce in your life, that will condemn or justify you in that great day.

CHAPTER FIVE

FAITH IS ESSENTIAL

"Without faith, it is impossible to please God!"

So says the apostle in He 11:6. Prayer is answered only if we please God. But we can please God only if we pray in faith. Why is this so?

THE REAL NECESSITY FOR FAITH

There are three reasons why faith is so necessary -

Faith Is Essential Because Without It We Are Naked

Faith is the only covering proper for us as we enter God's presence. Anything less than faith is disgraceful. Anything more than faith is arrogant.

Let me explain it this way. If you received an invitation to attend an official function at the Governor's mansion, the invitation would specify what kind of dress you should wear for the occasion. If you arrived improperly dressed, you would not be admitted.

In the same way God, exercising his divine prerogative, has decreed that he will accept us only when we are clothed with faith. Without faith it is impossible to please him. His pre-eminent demand is for faith. To approach him in unbelief is to insult his integrity. To approach him in self-righteousness is to despise his grace. Both attitudes display an obnoxious self-will instead of submission to his divine will.

But a great benefit arises from this demand for faith: it is one that any person can fulfil. Even the simplest and humblest of the children of God can come boldly into God's presence. A man's greatness will not give him any better access to God, neither will obscurity hinder his access. Personal merit has no effect. With faith, any person can come joyfully to the Lord; without it, no one can reach him.

Faith Is Essential Because Without It We Are False

The great statesman Benjamin Disraeli said, "Man is a being born to believe."[8] Indeed, the exercise of faith is one of the most important attributes (it may be the only one) that separates man from every other creature of God. Apart from God himself, faith is an attribute that probably belongs to man alone. Only man is able to exercise faith, and by faith to tap the inexhaustible riches of heaven.

Faith, then, is that which above all else distances man from the brute creation. Every other living creature is limited to the use of natural resources, or at least to those resources that are an inherent part of its nature. But man, by the right use of faith, can escape the limitations of his physical nature, and enter a realm where "nothing is impossible".

Hence the scripture says:

> *"All things are possible to him who believes"* ...
>
> *"Nothing will be impossible to you"* ...
>
> *"If you have faith, whatever you say will be done" (Mk 9:23; Mt 17:21; 21:21).*

Such promises have not been given to any other creature; not even to the angels (who act in the power of their own nature). They belong only to man. He alone can transcend every barrier of time, space, and natural law, and by faith achieve whatever God sets before him.

Thus Moses drove back the waters of the Red Sea, and Joshua held the sun still in the sky. Elijah and Elisha defied gravity, mocked death, and performed prodigious miracles. Christ walked on water, and multiplied a few loaves into a vast quantity of food. The disciples raised the dead, walked through prison doors, were

---

[8] Spoken in an address to Bishop Wilberforce, Oxford U.K., 1864. Disraeli was a British statesman who as Prime Minister purchased a controlling interest in the Suez Canal and made Queen Victoria the empress of India (1804-1881).

instantly transported from one place to another, and lived in a continual experience of the supernatural. All by faith, mighty faith.

Mind you, this does not mean that faith is always exemplified by obvious miracles, or that it can be demonstrated only by defiance of natural law. Faith may often be expressed in ways that seem to lack any supernatural content, yet the operation of divine power is no less present. That is why the writer to the Hebrews recorded some examples of faith that were plainly supernatural, and others that the world judged as proof that faith was invalid.

> He describes obviously supernatural events: "(Some) through faith conquered kingdoms, enforced justice, received promises, stopped the mouths of lions, quenched raging fire, escaped the edge of the sword, won strength out of weakness, became mighty in war, put foreign armies to flight, and women received their dead by resurrection."

> But he also describes seemingly natural events, that an unbeliever might construe as awful defeats for the people concerned: "Some (by faith) were tortured, refusing to accept release...others suffered mocking and scourging, and even chains and imprisonment. They were stoned, they were sawn in two, they were killed with the sword; they went about in skins of sheep and goats, destitute, afflicted, ill- treated...(but) well attested by their faith" (He 11:33-39).

Some died as an expression of their faith; some triumphed over death as an expression of their faith! Some by faith turned the sword aside, others by faith submitted themselves to the sword!

Faith in each case was equally victorious; for in each case faith enabled people to discover the will of God, and then successfully to complete his purpose for their lives. In each case that purpose involved the effective working of divine power; the events were all supernatural, whether or not they were recognised as such, **for no**

one can fulfil the will of God, whether it be to live or to die, without his mighty strength.

The task of faith is to find the will of God, and then bring that will to fruition. If that requires an act that does violence to natural law, or to ordinary physical limitations, then faith is ready for the challenge.

This principle was marvellously exemplified by Shadrach, Meshach, and Abednego. They were ready to believe either for a miracle of deliverance, or to die with calm courage:

> *"Our God whom we serve is able to deliver us from the burning fiery furnace; and he will deliver us...But if not, be it known to you, O king, that we will not serve your gods" (Da 3:17-18).*

All these things show that God has created man to live by faith, not by sight. We fulfil our true humanity only when faith becomes the governing principle of our lives. Without faith we are worthless. God's word to the man without faith has been from the beginning, and still is,

> *"You are dust, and to dust you shall return" (Ge 3:19).*

But to the believer he says:

> *"The righteous will shine like the sun in the kingdom of their Father. He who has ears, let him hear" (Mt 13:43).*

Faith Is Essential Because Without It We Are Disabled

Jesus said,

> *"God is spirit, and those who worship him must worship him in spirit and in truth" (Jn 4:24).*

But to worship in "spirit" means to worship in faith; for just as thought is the tool of the mind, and muscle the tool of the hand, so faith is the tool of the spirit:

> *"With the heart (spirit) man believes" (Ro 10:10).*

Faith provides impulse and strength to the human spirit. Without faith, the spirit is deaf, blind, paralysed, utterly incapacitated. Faith is the nerve centre and force behind all spiritual life. Without faith worship is an ugly mechanical ritual, a vain repetition of hollow sounds, a discordant jangle, a repulsive cacophony (Am 5:21; Pr 15:8; 28:9; Is 1:12-20; etc.)

THE REAL QUALITY OF FAITH

Faith is essentially two things: a matter of persuasion; and a divine impulse. Those two qualities are essential components of true faith. If the divine impulse is lacking, faith becomes a sterile intellectual exercise, a thing of the mind only, void of any supernatural character. But if faith is all impulse, without a basis of informed reason, it becomes an exercise in fanaticism, irrational and irresponsible, and antagonistic toward the true purpose of God.

Faith Is A Matter Of Persuasion

Many people have only a hazy notion of just what faith is. Faith is not a mysterious quality that we have to pull by some magical meanr out of the reluctant atmosphere. The primary meaning of the Greek word (*pistis*) translated "faith" in the Bible is simply "a firm persuasion", or "a strong conviction". Almost everywhere you see the word "faith" in the Bible you can put in its place "persuasion" or "persuaded".

So when you say that you have "faith in God" you are saying simply, "I am firmly convinced that certain things about God are true." What are these things that faith has been persuaded to believe?

Be Persuaded That There Is
A Promise To Cover Your Every Need

It has been claimed that the Bible contains some 3000 promises, covering every facet of human life. In this vast array of promises there is surely one that addresses your problem!

Your task is to approach the Bible with confidence that God will speak to you through its pages and show you his word for you at the present time.

Be Persuaded That God's Word Is Completely Reliable.

If faith is a matter of persuasion that God is true in what he says, it is easy to see why the Bible asserts, "without faith it is impossible to please him" - for to approach God without faith is just another way of saying you cannot believe what he says.

You resent being called a liar, and so does God:

> *"If we receive the testimony of men, the testimony of God is greater; for this is the testimony of God that he has borne witness to his Son. He who believes in the Son of God has the testimony in himself.[9] He who does not believe God has made him a liar, because he has not believed in the testimony that God has borne to his Son" (1 Jn 5:9-10).*

Those who believe the promise of God commit themselves to that promise. They have no doubt about its trustworthiness. Without reservation or anxiety they surrender fully to the authority of the word God has spoken. Having found a promise that meets their need, they claim that promise with whole-hearted confidence, being perfectly assured that God will do what he has promised to do.

The scripture is emphatic in its assertion that "God is able": he is able to heal every sickness; he is able to meet every financial need; he is able to give you health and prosperity; he is able to satisfy you with abundant life and happiness; he is able to keep you secure in his love until the day Jesus comes! He is able!"

---

[9] This is another passage of scripture that speaks about the evidential power of faith, that is, faith's inherent power to bear witness that the thing believed is true. As we saw in an earlier chapter: "He who believes, knows!"

Are you persuaded that he is able? Then you are close to great faith!

Be Persuaded That What You Have Asked For Is Already Done

Faith that cannot say, "I receive now! I have it now!" is not faith, but wishful thinking. I have already shown you that this is the kind of faith Christ demands:

> *"Whatever you desire, when you pray believe that you have received it, and you will receive it"* (Mk 11:24).

Accordingly, when you pray, you must at once believe that you receive what you ask for, and then you will have it. But if you cannot believe that you have already received it, then you probably won't get it!

This may seem to be the hardest part of faith, yet it is actually the easiest. It is hard only to unbelief. True faith almost unconsciously works by this principle. As John says, if we know that God has heard our prayers, then how can we help but know that we have received the petitions we desired of him? (1 Jn 5:14-15).

When the Lord has promised to give you some good thing, and you ask him to fulfil that promise, it is only reasonable for you to be confident that he heard you the moment you prayed, and granted your request. If you lack this confidence, how can you please him?

There may be a little delay before the benefit you are seeking comes your way - that is, before it assumes a tangible form. But that is no reason for doubt about the genuineness of the promise nor about the ability of God to fulfil it.

We are told to "hold fast to our faith without wavering", knowing that when we ask according to God's will he does hear us, and immediately grants our request. But if we keep on praying and praying, full of doubt and uncertainty, we cannot reasonably expect an answer to our prayer.

I do not mean that you cannot pray more than once. Pray as many times as you feel the need to pray. But let it be in faith. Or if you cannot pray in faith, then pray for faith. But never should you pray in doubt (Ja 1:6-8). Even when prayer is wrought in anguish (as Jesus prayed in the garden, Lu 22:44), even when it is drenched with tears, it should still throb with faith. There can never be any justifiable reason for a believer to pray in unbelief.

Faith Is A Divine Impulse

To say that faith is a matter of persuasion is to tell only half of faith's quality. For to stop there reduces faith to mere intellectual comprehension. It becomes a thing of the mind only, and not of the heart.

But faith is much more than mental mechanics. It is indeed based on sound thinking, and on a proper understanding of the word of God. It cannot exist apart from a firm persuasion that God's word is true. But neither can it stop there. Just as Adam did not become "a living soul" until God breathed life into him, so faith needs that same divine breath to change it from a thing of dust to a thing of living beauty and power.

Hence the scriptures describe faith as a gift of God, as a gift of the Holy Spirit, and also as a fruit of the ministry of the Spirit in our lives.

So the faith I am discussing in this book is much more than the kind of trust that people express toward each other in everyday life. This faith that pleases God is not just a religious variation of the confidence we show in a carpenter when we sit in his chair.

Godly faith does ring with confidence, and it is certainly trustful. But it has also a spiritual quality, which takes it beyond the realm of merely natural belief, or of ordinary assurance, into a charismatic dimension, one that is inaccessible without Divine assistance.

No one can believe unless God gives it to him to believe. No one can believe beyond the measure of faith God has assigned him.

Our responsibility is to open our hearts to the ministry of the Spirit, to approach God's word, and God himself, with sincerity, confident that faith will be born within us, yet willing to accept what limitation the Lord may impose on the exercise of our faith.

So Paul writes:

> *"(You must) think with sober judgment, each according to the measure of faith that God has assigned him ...Having gifts that differ according to the grace given to us, let us use them...in proportion to our faith" (Ro 12:3, 6).*

To each person God has given, or is willing to give, a measure of faith. That measure is not the same for all of us. It comes from the grace of God, and accords with his purpose for our lives. Hence we can serve God only "in proportion to our faith". However, most of us are not in much peril of exceeding our faith-capacity, even if it is small. We are more prone not to realise our full potential!

I will have served you well if this book helps you to discover the areas in which God is wanting you to use faith, and then to release your faith to its fullest measure, so that his purpose for you will be perfected.

THE REAL FOCUS OF FAITH

> *"Without faith it is impossible to please God!" (He 11:6).*

It is difficult to convey in English how strong that declaration is in Greek, but let me attempt a paraphrase: "You will be quite unable to bring God any pleasure, no matter what you do, or how or when you do it, unless you have faith!"

Plainly, this demand for faith is unavoidable. Faith has no substitute that you can offer and still hope to please God. If you want bold access to heaven's throne, you had better come with faith!

Which leaves the apostle with no choice except to affirm: "If you would come to God, then you MUST believe!" Once again his language is singularly strong. He uses a powerful imperative - you must believe, you simply and absolutely **must**!

The Greek word is ***"dei"***, which is more emphatic even than the English "must". In the pagan world, *"dei"* was associated with the irresistible power of Fate, that mysterious force before which all gods and men had to yield. Not even mighty Zeus, the Lord of Olympus, could escape the decrees of Fate.

Herodotus illustrates the force of *"dei"* in his story of the fabulously wealthy Croesus, the king of Lydia. Croesus was hungry to expand his dominion, so he decided to attack Persia. But first he craved a favorable word from heaven. So he sent an array of magnificent gifts to the oracle at Delphi in the hope of buying the support of the gods. He was told that if he attacked Persia he would "destroy a great empire". Much encouraged he went to war, and was mauled by the Persians. He had failed to ask **which** empire would fall!

In great bitterness he sent a message to the oracle, complaining that he had been deceived. The Priestess replied that not even the highest of the gods could escape the destiny ordained for all living things. Every person's fate was predetermined, and no gift or sacrifice could alter what was decreed.

So this is the sense of *"dei"* as the Greeks used it: it was associated with anything that was seen to be a fixed necessity or an irresistible purpose. It described an unchangeable fact, an invincible authority. It represented whatever was absolutely unshakeable in force or will.

The early Christians took hold of *"dei"* and added to it the special meaning of "a divine imperative" - that is, something decreed by the immutable, indestructible, unalterable will of God. Hence it is used by John:

> *"The revelation of Jesus Christ, which God gave him to show his servants what must (dei) soon take place" (Re 1:1).*

Nothing in heaven, on earth, or in hell can prevent what God has spoken from happening!

So that is the word found in our text: "You must believe!"

The sense is: "Before you even **begin** to draw near to God, you must, you simply **must** get your faith into good order." Unless you do, there is no hope of pleasing God.

But what does "get your faith into good order" mean? The apostle declares that faith must begin by believing three things -

Faith Believes That God "Exists"

The original text (He 11:6) is really more forthright. It reads literally, "Believe that God is!" Not merely that he has existence, but that he is truly present in your now, at the very heart of your situation, at the centre of your circumstances, not far distant, but closer to you than your own flesh -

> *Speak to Him thou for he hears,*
>
> *and spirit with Spirit can meet*
>
> *- Closer is He than breathing,*
>
> *and nearer than hands and feet*[10]

God is! He is now! He is real! He is near at hand! He is attentive to your prayer! He is able! He is concerned about you! He is interested in your welfare! He is merciful and kind! He is Saviour and Healer! He is not tomorrow but **today**! He is the same yesterday, today, and forever! He is willing to answer your prayer, and to bring you your heart's desires.

On one occasion the Lord God rebuked Israel because the people thought that he was restricted to only one place; they did not realise that he was everywhere: "Can anyone hide in secret places so that I cannot see him?" declares the Lord.

> *"Do I not fill heaven and earth?" declares the Lord! (Je 23:23-24).*

---

[10] Alfred, Lord Tennyson, "The Higher Pantheism," st. 6.

There is a demand in that passage for us to live with an awareness of God's presence. Indeed, real faith, miracle-working faith, will hardly be possible without such an awareness. But let a believer have a deep sense of God's nearness and it will hardly be possible to pray without faith!

We have been taught to walk "by faith, not by sight" - that is, not to need nor to depend upon any **experience** of God's presence. There is, of course, much truth in that teaching. Sometimes God himself will test our faith by withdrawing from us (or at least by **seeming** to withdraw). But to live constantly without any feeling of God, and to be content with such a state, is actually a **failure** of faith, not a triumph.

True faith will certainly continue to believe, whether or not God seems to be near; **but true faith will also strive vigorously to regain an awareness of God.** It can never be satisfied to walk in perpetual darkness. It hungers to hold God's hand. It yearns to see, or at least to sense, the beauty of the Lord (cp. Ps 27:4-5; and notice, in vs. 6, how the psalmist reckoned that victory would be his after he had met with God).

How fervently godly people pleaded with the Lord to restore his presence to them! What anguish gripped their souls when it seemed that their God had forsaken them. How bitterly and urgently they cried out for him to clothe them once again with his glory! (See Ps 22:1; 51:9-11; 139:7-10; etc.)

It is hardly an accident that our text ("Without faith it is impossible to please God") follows hard upon the story of one of the great pleasers of God in scripture, Enoch, the man who **walked with God**! So close was his fellowship with the Father, and so great was his faith as a consequence, that he escaped death and was raptured into heaven.

A close walk and mighty faith are inseparable.

Thus irresistible faith begins here: it believes that God **is**; it comes into the presence of God; it steps right up to the throne; it speaks to God, not far away, but near at hand.

Faith Believes That God "Rewards"

"If you come to God, you must believe that he is, and that he is the Rewarder of those who diligently seek him." (He 11:6)

The apostle uses here another arresting word, "Rewarder". The original word, in the Greek text, is unique. Prior to this occurrence it has not been found in any other ancient Greek writing. So it seems to have been coined by the apostle himself.

It is as though he was striving to express a wonderful idea about God, but could not find an existing word to satisfy his thought, so he invented a new one. He put together three words to form a compound noun that means literally, "he who pays back a generous wage." It has the sense of "one who gives richly"; or, "one who rewards bountifully."

Notice that the word is a noun, not a verb (as it is translated in some versions). He did not say merely that God "rewards", but rather that God's very name and nature is "Rewarder". He is giving us a new name for God. We already call him Father, Saviour, Healer, Redeemer - now we can also call him **Rewarder**.

Furthermore, he links this name with a verbal structure that conveys the idea of continuity. That is, God is not just an **occasional** Rewarder; rather, it is his **habit** to reward those who seek him. He continually proves himself to be the Rewarder. He is always showing himself in that character. He can never be any other.

Faith perceives this. Faith rejoices in it. Faith depends upon it. Faith never doubts that there is a vast generosity in God.

Faith expects its rich wages - the bounty of the Lord given magnificently in answer to believing prayer!

Unhappily, most people have a problem with that concept - either because they have a poor opinion of themselves, or a poor opinion of God, or both...

They Have A Poor Opinion Of Themselves

There are times when it is proper for us to be downcast because of our sins, and to approach God contritely, even with tears, to seek his pardon. It is equally certain that we dare not remain in that state. We are commanded to trust the promise (1 Jn1:9), to know that all sin is forgiven, and then to come boldly to the throne of grace (He 4:16). Nothing in scripture requires a believer to remain in a state of breast-beating despair. Indeed, to do so is to insult the grace of God and to despise his promise.

There is a marvellous saying of Paul's:

> *"God has **blessed** us in the heavenlies with every spiritual blessing in Christ" (Ep 1:3).*

Our word "eulogy" comes from the Greek word that is translated "blessed" in that passage. Both words have the same basic meaning: "to speak well of someone".

Up there, in the heavenlies, what is God saying about you? Is he denouncing you, calling you a miserable worm, worthless flotsam, vile sewage? Is he angrily planning how he can best punish you? Does he watch for every opportunity to do you some mischief? Is he just waiting for you to pray so that he can spitefully refuse to bless you?

Some people expect such an attitude from God because that is how they think about themselves. But if you have truly repented of your sins, and have trusted in the blood of the everlasting covenant, then you have a right to think as well of yourself as God does.

Paul is emphatic. He says that God is speaking well of you in heaven. But now you must respond by speaking well of yourself on earth. Your opinion on this matter, as on every matter, must echo the opinion of God. To do otherwise is to make God a liar - which is hardly the way to please him.

Because God has a high opinion of you in Christ, every spiritual blessing is properly yours - that is, you have a right to claim the fulfilment of every promise that belongs to you. But you will never be bold enough to lodge that claim so long as you keep on speaking poorly about one whom God has "eulogised"!

Learn then to say about yourself what God says. Because you have come into union with Christ through faith, the Father speaks well of you, and desires to enrich you with every blessing contained in his wide promise.

They Have A Poor Opinion Of God

Honestly, what name do you give God in your deepest spirit? Do you echo the excited cry of the apostle: "I call him my Rewarder"? Or would you more truthfully call him "Niggard" - an ancient title for a stingy and close-fisted miser?

Or there is another term that aptly describes the opinion some people have about God. If they dared, they would call him "Skinflint" - a piece of thieve's slang for a person so mean that he would try to skin a flint just to save a few pennies!

Is that how you feel about the Father? Or do you truly expect him to overflow with generosity and kindness, rewarding you bountifully when you seek him?

Martin Luther put this same challenge to his listeners, and sternly rebuked those who had scant expectation of great answers to their prayers:

> (God) wants the honor of giving far more abundantly and richly than anyone can comprehend; like an eternal, unfailing fountain, the more it gushes forth and overflows, the more it continues to supply. And he desires nothing more earnestly of us than that we ask many and great things of him, and he is angry if we do not pray and petition with confidence.
>
> If the richest and most powerful emperor were to bid a poor beggar ask for whatever he might desire and

were ready to give great, princely presents, but the fool were to beg only for a serving of common soup, he would justly be considered a rogue and a scoundrel, who made the command of His Imperial Majesty the object of mockery and derision and was not worthy to come into his presence.

In like manner, it is a disgrace and dishonor to God if we, to whom he offers and promises so many unspeakable blessings, despise them or are not confident that we shall receive them, and if we scarcely venture to ask for a morsel of bread.[11]

We have now seen the first two parts of the kind of faith that pleases God. But there is a third thing that we must believe -

Faith Believes That God "Delays"

By now (especially after reading Luther's anecdote) you may be protesting, "But I **have been** asking God for golden blessings, yet I have not even been given a bowl of soup!"

That is indeed a perplexing problem. It is probably impossible, if you commit yourself to pray great prayers and to expect great things, not to experience the frustration of seeming to be ignored by an indifferent heaven. I do not have all of the answers to that problem; but one important clue is given in our text (He 11:6) -

Anyone who comes to God must believe that he is the Rewarder of those who **seek him diligently**.

Note, he rewards not those who merely seek him, but rather those who **diligently** seek him. Once again, in a passage full of strong words, this word is also strong. The Greek verb is an intensified form of an ordinary expression meaning "look for" or "ask for" - as

---

[11] From What Luther Says, Vol II, #3510; compiled by E. W. Plass; Concordia Publishing House, Saint Louis, Missouri; 1959

though the apostle had written it like some of the words in this study, in italics and underlined!

This "diligence" in prayer demands two things -

Persistence

The idea has sometimes been suggested that if you pray for something more than once, then every prayer except the last must have been in unbelief. I can find no warrant in scripture for arguing that faith will be content to pray but once, and no more.

On the contrary, Jesus himself linked **faith** with **persistent** prayer - see Lu 18:1-8.

He taught the same idea in his famous saying about "asking, seeking, and knocking" (Lu 11:9-10). There is a rising intensity in the three verbs, moving from ask, to **seek**, to **knock**; and there is a demand for constant, persistent prayer in his use of the present continuous tense, which could be translated: "ask, **and keep on asking; seek,** and keep on seeking; knock, **and keep on knocking.**" The sense of the passage is simply, if your prayer is not granted when you **ask**, then begin to seek; and if it is not answered when you **seek**, then begin to knock; and if it is still not answered after you **knock**, then keep on doing all three until it **is** answered!

The reason for all this lies in the mystery of God's providence: sometimes the Father chooses to delay the answers we so earnestly desire. We may or may not discover the reasons for that delay. But in any case, faith will continue in prayer, refusing to allow any tardiness, whether short or long, to undermine its confident boast that God **is** the Rewarder of those who persistently seek him. After all, if prayer were always answered instantly, there would be no point in promising a special reward to the diligent.

Patience

Faith hardly ever stands alone. Almost always it is associated with other words. One of them (as we have just seen) is "persistence", and another is "patience" - see He 10:35-39; 6:12.

If the promise delays - and there will certainly be times when it **will** delay - then wait for it! Do not act hastily, as Abraham did, and produce an "Ishmael" to be a constant embarrassment and pain to you. There is only one way to walk with God, and that is to walk **with** him. If you run ahead you will run alone. If you scamper off impatiently to this side or that, you will be isolated away from his help.

While you persevere in prayer, learn also to hold your spirit firm in unworried trust.

You may never know why God chooses to delay the answer to this prayer or that, or why his promise sometimes seems so sluggish in fulfilment, but you can be quite sure that such delays are a normal part of the life of faith. Through them the Lord is working out his own good purpose. If you continue to call the Lord your Shepherd, whether he is leading you through green pastures or through the shadowed valley of death, you will eventually discover, as did the psalmist, all the riches of his goodness and mercy, and you will dwell in his house for ever.

Faith brings a great reward. But only to those **"who believe that God exists, and that he is the Rewarder of those who diligently seek him!"**

CHAPTER SIX

WORDS THAT WORK MIRACLES

"For this saying you may go your way; the demon has left your daughter" (Mk 7:29).

SAYING THE RIGHT THING

What power words have!

How forceful are right words!

The woman in our text addressed herself to Jesus in a way that compelled his response and brought deliverance to her daughter. Her words were so irresistible that not even a demon could hide from their impact. She spoke, and a miracle happened!

Christ confirmed that her words had moved him to action. He said to her, **"For this saying... your daughter is made well."**

For another saying she might well have gained no response from Christ. She might even have stirred him to anger. But her words were right; they were bold words of faith; the Master could not resist them; so he gave her her heart's desire.

To silence, Christ could not have responded; to a wrong saying he would not have responded; but a right saying drew from him a loving and powerful response, and a miracle that turned the impossible into the possible.

This fact must be faced: there is no substitute for speaking aloud the word of faith. Thinking it, wishing it, hoping it, breathing it, is not enough - **you must speak it!**

Your spoken word is the catalyst that triggers the promise of God into action. Without that spoken word the promise may remain dormant and unfulfilled in your life. But if you learn to say the right thing in the right way at the right time, then you will find yourself linked with the same awesome power that enabled Joshua to stop the progress of the sun, or Samuel to cause the thunder to roar from heaven, or Elijah to raise the dead, or Paul to shake off a viper.

The rule of faith is emphatic: for **"this"** saying the Lord will hear you, for **"that"** saying he may not hear you; for "this" saying you will gain a miracle, for "that" saying you will be denied a miracle; for "this" saying you have gained the favor of God, for that saying his face is turned from you.

Remember that Jesus said: *"by your words you will be justified, and by your words you will be condemned."* (Mt 12:37). The words you speak play a crucial part in determining whether or not you will gain divine acceptance. A confession of faith will justify you; a confession of unbelief will condemn you.

But there is something more here. The lesser is always included in the greater. So if the great issues of justification and condemnation depend on the words you speak, how much more dependent on your words are the lesser issues of your daily life!

There is no evading this spiritual law. For this saying your financial need will be met; for that saying it will not be met. For this saying you will be healed; for that saying you will remain ill. For this saying you will conquer a habit; for that saying you will remain defeated. For this saying your prayer will be answered; for that saying it will not be answered ... and so on.

What do you think the Lord's response is to the things that you are saying day by day?

THE FINAL STAGE OF FAITH

There are three stages in the development of faith (see Ro 10:8-17)

> getting the promise of God into your head, through searching the scriptures, and by prayer; for faith cannot exist apart from a word from God.

> getting the promise of God into your heart, through divine revelation, so that it becomes quickened in your spirit, alive and powerful.
>
> getting the word of God onto your lips, through boldly speaking it aloud.

For most people, that third stage is probably the most difficult. Not because they cannot say the right words, but because they do not really have any confidence that what they say will come to pass. They feel foolish, talking to nothing, or to inanimate things!

It may be alright for Jesus to issue commands to the wind and the waves, or to fig trees, sycamore trees, and mountains; but somehow it seems silly when we try to do it. Yet Christ left us no choice in the matter. We are required to express our faith exactly as he did - by speaking directly to the Situation we want changed ...

Mountain Movers

Mark well these sayings of the Master -

> *(1) "For truly, I say to you, if you have faith as a grain of mustard seed, you will say to this mountain, 'Move hence to yonder place,' and it will move; and nothing will be impossible to you" (Mt 17:20).*

Notice, he did not say, "nothing will be impossible to God", but "nothing will be impossible to you!"

That promise, however, can be realised only if you are bold enough to stand in front of your mountain and actually speak to it, never doubting that it will obey your voice and do just as you say. Nor do you need a lot of faith, nor any special kind of faith. All you need is faith. Faith cannot be qualified. The point of Jesus' reference to "faith as a grain of mustard seed" is simply that you must have faith. You either have it or you don't. If you do have it, then you will speak it; for it is in the very nature of faith to be released, to be sprung into action by the spoken word.

> *(2) "Truly, I say to you, if you have faith and never doubt, you will not only do what has been done to the fig tree, but even if you say to this mountain, `Be taken up and cast into the sea,' it will be done. And whatever you ask in prayer, you will receive, if you have faith" (Mt 21:18-22).*

Jesus said, "I spoke to a fig tree, and it obeyed me; but that is a small thing - you can speak to a mountain, and it will do as you say!"

But it will only do it if you say it. If there is no saying there will be no doing. "For this saying" the mountain will move; but otherwise it will stay right where it is!

You may ask, "How could Christ possibly give such power to fallen sinners? Surely he did not really mean that nothing is impossible to us?" Yes, he meant exactly what he said, for there is an all-important qualifier: "if you have faith". You can move mountains, you can do anything at all by speaking a word of command, only if you have faith. But it is impossible to have faith apart from a word from God. Faith cannot exist unless it springs out of a promise God has given. So find out what God has to say about your situation, get a promise from him, let that promise become vibrantly alive in your heart; then faith will be born within you, waiting to create your miracle the moment you speak the word!

> *(3) "Have faith in God. Truly, I say to you, whoever says to this mountain, `Be taken up and cast into the sea,' and does not doubt in his heart, but believes that what he says will come to pass, it will be done for him" (Mk 11:23).*

Notice that your chief enemy is doubt. Whoever wants to live in this dimension of miracle-working faith must do something about doubt. Perhaps that is the first mountain that must be moved! By prayer, by saturating your spirit with the word of God, by self discipline, by any other means, you must eradicate all doubt - for only "if you have faith and never doubt" will your voice have power to compel mountains to move.

Quantity Or Quality?

> *"The apostles said to the Lord, `Increase our faith!'  And the Lord said, `If you had faith as a grain of mustard seed, you could say to this sycamine tree, "Be rooted up, and be planted in the sea", and it would obey you'" (Lu 17:5-6).*

It is evident that Jesus repeated the above lesson on several different occasions. It was an important lesson, one that the apostles were slow to grasp, so the Lord seized every opportunity to drive it into their spirits.

Notice also how the disciples were concerned about the quantity of faith; they wanted more of it. But Christ was not concerned about this. Whether they had more faith or less was unimportant. Only one thing was important: did they or did they not have faith? If they had faith, genuine faith, even if only as a grain of mustard seed, nothing would lie beyond their power.[12]

Nonetheless, all faith, whether great or small, remains dormant until it is expressed in a word of command or of affirmation. So the real task of the disciples (as it is also ours) was simply to get faith into their hearts, and then onto their lips. It is the merging of these two

---

[12] The old 17th century German commentator, John Bengel, offers a lively comment on "mustard seed faith". On Mt 17-20 he writes: "It is clear that the transportation of a mountain is a less miracle than the ejection of a devil of the kind mentioned in the text; for the devil clings more closely to a man spiritually than a mountain to its roots physically; and faith, even the smallest, is more powerful than the fixture of a mountain. Do you say, Why then is that the less frequent miracle? I reply, It has nevertheless been sometimes wrought; but it is not often necessary, although the opulence of faith reaches thus far. A mountain is naturally by creation in its proper place; a devil is not so in a man: hence it is more beneficial to cast him out than to remove the mountain." (New Testament Word Studies; 1971 reprint by Kregel Publications, Grand Rapids, Michigan; Vol. 1. pg. 221.

things - inner belief and bold speech - that unlocks the miracle-working power of God. Hence the apostle said:

> *"For man believes with his heart and so is justified,*
> *and he confesses with his lips and so is saved"*
> *(Ro 10:10).*

Paul there applies the principle of heart belief/mouth confession to the great issue of salvation. But as I have already suggested, lesser benefits are naturally included in the greater; so what applies to salvation applies also to every benefit you desire to receive from God.

Notice also that the very word for "**salvation**" in the Greek text ("*soteria*") means far more than just pardon of sin and rescue from the coming judgment. It embraces an exciting gamut of ideas - from personal safety, to good health, to prosperity, to deliverance, and so on. It describes a perfect and complete salvation/healing of your entire being - body, soul, and spirit. But your spoken confession is an integral part of the faith-combination that unlocks the door to that all-encompassing salvation.[13]

The electronic wizardry of our time includes a gadget that will lock or unlock a door in response to the human voice. It can also be used to switch lights on or off, and to operate many other pieces of domestic equipment. You simply walk up to a door, command it to open, and presto! it obeys. Or you walk into a dark room, command the light to shine, and behold! there is light. This gadget can also be set so that it will obey only one person's voice and no other. Every human being, it has been discovered, has a unique voice pattern. Just as your fingerprint differs from that of any other person who has ever lived, so does the electronic pattern of your voice. Thus a door or a light operated by this gadget can be adjusted to respond to your voice alone.

---

[13] The wide meaning of "*soteria*" and its associated verb "*sozo*" is discussed more fully in the series of chapters on Divine Healing.

In some respects the promises of God are like that. They are so structured that only the sound of the human voice can galvanise them into action. And in particular, it is the sound of your voice that will make the promises operative in your life.

The scripture means exactly what it says: "confess it with your lips, and you will be saved" - which includes full deliverance, abundant life, and all the good things that God wants to give you in Christ.

MAKING THE PROMISE EFFECTIVE

> *"God has said, `I will never fail you nor forsake you.' Hence we can confidently say, `The Lord is my helper, I will not be afraid; what can man do to me?'" (He 13:5-6).*

Here are two important principles -

Personalising The Promise

The promises of God are usually phrased in broad and general terms, so that they can be appropriated by the largest number of people. But the appropriation of a promise, to be truly effective, needs to be personalised and related closely to your particular situation and need.

Hence, in the example above, the apostle

> takes a general promise: "I will never fail you nor forsake you;"
>
> then he personalises it: "**The Lord is my helper**;"
>
> then he applies it: "I will not be afraid; what can man do to me?" (He 13:5b-6).)

The general promise, as it stands, is too broad to be truly meaningful in a particular life situation. Its scope must be narrowed. It must be brought into focus on the need you currently face. Its force must be concentrated onto one problem.

Your faith will be quickened if you follow this procedure: identify your need; find a promise pertinent to that need; rephrase the promise so that your need is specifically mentioned; then boldly apply the promise to your need.

An example follows:

(1) Broad promise:

> "My God will supply every need of yours according to his riches in glory in Christ Jesus" (Ph 4:19).

(2) Need identified:

> "I am out of work and must find employment."

(3) Promise personalised:

> "My God knows the kind of job I need, he knows just where to find that job, he is able to direct me to it and to secure it for me."

(4) Promise applied:

> "I will trust the Lord to help me find a job, and to care for me. In the meantime, I will not be afraid, nor doubt that he is acting on my behalf with all wisdom, skill, and power."

Another example:

(1) Broad promise:

> "For God so loved the world, he gave his only Son, that whoever believes in him should not perish but have eternal life" (Jn 3:16).

(2) Need identified:

> "I am a sinner, doomed to perish unless God in mercy intervenes."

(3) Promise personalised:

> "God so loved me he gave his only Son, so that I might believe in Christ and not perish, but have eternal life."

(4) Promise applied:

> *"I resolve to believe in Christ; and I accept him as Lord and Saviour, knowing that God has forgiven my sin and given me eternal life. I am no longer afraid of death nor of the judgment to follow."*

You could follow the same faith-generating, faith-releasing procedure with any of the promises of God.

PRONOUNCING THE PROMISE

As well as personalising the promise, you must also pronounce it. God's word has to be matched by your word.

The apostle quotes God, "He has said, 'I will never fail you!'" But if God has spoken, then you also must speak. The only proper response to God's word is a word response. So, having told us what God has said, the apostle at once continues: "Hence we can confidently say, 'The Lord is my helper, I will not be afraid!'"

Whenever God gives a promise to his people, he looks for a bold affirmation to be returned to him.

If God says to me, *"I will take sickness away from the midst of you"* (Ex 23:25), then I must boldly say, **"Lord, you are healing my arthritis (or whatever) right now!"**

If God says to me, *"You can do all things in Christ who strengthens you"* (Ph 4:13), then I must boldly say, **"In Christ I am well able to cope with my problem. I will rise above it in Jesus' name and not be harmed by it!"**

If God says to me, *"You are strengthened with might through my Spirit in the inner man"* (Ep 3:16), then I must boldly say, **"By his Spirit I am victorious over every sin; no habit can bind me; I am living in the victory of God!"**

If God says to me, *"I am the Lord your Shepherd, you shall not want,"* (Ps 23:1), then I must boldly say, **"God is with me in this difficult situation; he brought me into it, he will take me out of it; and whatever I need he will give me!"**

Your bold saying of the promise is the trigger that releases the power of the promise into your life. But do you really have to say it aloud? Why can't you just think it? Why must it be spoken? What is the difference between *thinking* the promise and speaking it?

Simply this: "out of the abundance of the heart the mouth speaks" (Mt 12:34). If you are reluctant to speak the promise, to say it aloud, to declare boldly your confidence in it, then you are showing that, deep down, you probably don't believe it.

If you have an abundant faith in your heart, you will have a bold confession on your lips. The two belong together as naturally as sunshine and summer, as closely as a flower and its fragrance. "I believed, therefore have I spoken." This is an inevitable description of the man of faith: he who believes, speaks!

FASCINATING WORDS OF FAITH

In the remainder of this Chapter I want to explore several special words that are found in the New Testament. Each of these words exposes a new and fascinating aspect of faith. Each different facet sparkles with light and beauty, and together they help to build a composite picture of faith, one that is full of life and power.

The texts are not selected in any particular order. I have dealt with them just as they have come to hand.

Confession - "*Homologia*"

This word is a compound of two others that mean "alike words", hence (in its verb form), "to speak the same thing", "to adopt the same style of speech", "to speak alike", "to speak with accord"; and so on. In our case, "*homologia*" means "saying the same thing God says", "speaking according to his word".

"*Homologia*" is used in He 3:1 –

> "*Therefore, holy brethren, who share in a heavenly call, consider Jesus, the apostle and high priest of our confession.*"

In connection with prayer and the miracle-working power of God, that verse is one of the most vital in the Bible. It says that God has chosen Christ to be our apostle and high priest.

As our apostle, Christ has been given power to act on our behalf, to meet every need, and to bring us to an experience of the full range of God's mercy and kindness.

As our high priest, Christ has been given the right to make a sacrifice on our behalf and to intercede for us before the Father's throne.

We have dire need of those two things. We need someone who can obliterate our guilt, impute righteousness to us, and reconcile us to God. And we need someone who has power to smash the chains of sin and sickness, and to free us to serve God with joy. Christ has that power. He can loose you from every bondage, and he can restore you to fellowship with the Father. He can do those things, because God has made him apostle and high priest to all who believe.

But there is one vital condition. The text says that he is apostle and high priest *"of our confession"*. In other words, Christ will act as apostle and high priest for you only as you make a proper confession of faith. The things you say and the way you say them are the key to this wonderful ministry of Christ. He administers what you say with your lips, whether for good or ill - *"He has power to help, or power to cast down"* (2 Ch 25:8).

You may have faith in your heart, but if you make a wrong confession you will get the wrong answer, because Christ is the apostle of your confession.

You will often hear the encouragement, *"Hold fast to your faith."* But the scripture more frequently urges the duty of holding fast to the confession of your faith. We are in more danger of losing grip on the confession of faith than we are of losing faith itself (although in point of fact, to lose one will eventually lead to the loss of the other).

Hence we read -

> *"Since we have a great high priest who has passed through the heavens, Jesus, the Son of God, let us hold fast our confession" (He 4:14) ... "Let us hold fast the confession of our hope without wavering, for he who promised is faithful" (10:23) ... "Follow the pattern of the sound words which you have heard" (2 Ti 1:13).*

The sound words God has spoken to us - that is the pattern we should follow. To confess what God confesses; to allow no discord to develop between his words and yours - that is what it means to hold fast to your confession of faith.

The Lord, the apostle and high priest of our confession, promises this: if you speak in accordance with his word before men, he will speak in accordance with your word before the Father (Mt 10:32, where "**confession**" is once again "*homologeo*").

When the words you speak blend in confident harmony with the words God speaks, when your words are a vigorous expression of the faith that is in your heart - that is when Christ will transform your words into an instrument of his power, invincible, creative, calling into existence the things you speak.

Doubt - "*Diakrino*"

Leo Harris writes -

It's so easy to say, "**I believe**".

We don't really know what we actually do believe, however, until the pressure is applied.

Anyone who thinks it is easy to believe has not launched out very far in the exercise of his believing-power.

I have often said, "**We only really possess what we can hold under pressure.**" The same rule applies to our believing.

We only really believe what we continue to believe unwaveringly under pressure.

There are certainly some basic problems in this matter of believing.

THE GREEKS HAD A WORD

A study of the New Testament reveals that the Greeks had a word for one of the major problems in believing.

It is "*diakrino*".

Used 19 times in the Greek New Testament, "*diakrino*" has been translated in our King James Bible as to judge, reason, waver, stagger, discern, make a difference, and doubt. "*Diakrino*" is not necessarily a bad thing, in fact, it is sometimes a very wise and good thing. It is a problem only when it runs counter to our believing. This word, translated in various ways as shown, involves a mental debating, weighing pros and cons. I want to examine three usages of "*diakrino*" in relation to our believing.

DOUBT BEFORE A MOUNTAIN

Jesus said,

> *"If you have faith, and doubt (diakrino) not...you shall say unto this mountain, Be thou removed, and be thou cast into the sea; and it shall be done" (Mt 21:21).*

I have yet to find the person, who, in his right mind, would command Mt. Kosciusko to be cast into the Pacific Ocean!

And this is, no doubt, the beneficial aspect of "*diakrino*" - a safeguard against fanatics attempting that which is crazy, or morally wrong.

However, on the other hand, "*diakrino*" can be a basic problem in believing. Your "**mountain**" may be a sickness, a financial need, a business problem; but as you face this "**mountain**" you doubt the possibility of its removal. You have faith, or at least a faith-potential, but in your believing there is this "*diakrino*". Jesus confirmed his conditional promise in the very next verse: *"And all things,* *whatsoever you shall ask in prayer, believing, you shall receive"* (Mt 21:22).

The condition is our believing!

STAGGERING BEFORE IMPOSSIBILITIES

To Abraham God had promised descendants innumerable as the stars of heaven or the sand of the seashore. What made this mammoth task impossible was the fact that God also stipulated that this multitudinous race would come through the as – yet - unborn Isaac; and Abraham and Sarah were virtually centenarians!

"Oh God," he might have cried, **"if we could only get started on this vast project - just one little baby."** But then he would look up at the stars, kick his feet in the sand - and remember God's promise.

> *"And being not weak in faith, he considered not his own body now dead when he was about a hundred years old, neither yet the deadness of Sarah's womb. He staggered not at the promise of God through unbelief; but was strong in faith, giving glory to God; and being fully persuaded that what he had promised, he was able also to perform." (Ro. 4:19-21).*

Isaac was born, and a great race sprang forth!

"Staggered" is translated from *"diakrino"*. But see how Abraham's believing was undergirded so that he should not fall to this *"diakrino"* of staggering before the impossibility - Abraham **"considered not"** the contrary evidence in his own body; he was **"fully persuaded"** that God could perform his promise; so he **"staggered not"** in his believing.

And that's how your **"Isaac"** will be brought into being!

WAVERING BEFORE CIRCUMSTANCES

> *"**Let him ask in faith**", said James, "nothing wavering. For he who wavers is like a wave of the*

sea driven with the wind and tossed. For let not that man think he shall receive anything of the Lord. A double minded man is unstable in all his ways" (Ja 1:6-8).

Here our word *"diakrino"* is translated "**wavering**". The picture painted for us is of a man who begins well. He asks in faith. But contrary winds blow. Circumstances change. Opposite opinions are heard. Adverse reports are received. Symptoms flare up. Instead of holding his believing firm and steadfast, he allows it to become blown about like a wave of the sea. He becomes double minded. He wavers.

"Diakrino!"

And James adds those sobering words: *"Let not that man think that he shall receive anything of the Lord."* He asked in faith - but was defeated by *"diakrino"*.

RIGHT AND WRONG BELIEVING

We should remember that believing can be a two-way operation. We can believe the right way or the wrong way. *"Diakrino"* expresses the conflict, the debating between right and wrong believing.

Fear is wrong believing.

So is confusion, worry, resentment, self-pity, and doubt.

Right believing is taking God at his word, and committing ourselves to his promises - without doubting, without staggering, without wavering.

Our believing-power has limitless possibilities, if we can avoid the problem of *"diakrino"* by the discipline of our thoughts, attitudes and emotions.

The key is in the renewing of our minds, conditioning them by the Word of God. To do this we must familiarise ourselves with God's promises, allowing the Holy Spirit to make them alive and meaningful to us - think them, rejoice in them, openly confess them - and hold our believing firm to the end.

May we all learn how to believe and receive, for the glory of God.[14]

In contrast with Bengel,[15] who accepts the statement literally, it is astonishing to find many commentators who back away from what Jesus actually said and try to give it a lesser meaning. The following extract is typical: "When Jesus spoke about 'removing mountains' he was using a phrase which the Jews knew well. A great teacher, who could really expound and interpret scripture, and who could explain and resolve difficulties, was regularly known as an 'uprooter' or, even a 'pulverizer' of mountains. To tear up, to uproot, to pulverize mountains were all regular phrases for removing difficulties."

Perhaps what that commentator says is partly true; but it seems unlikely that Jesus intended nothing more than a proverbial saying about solving literary problems. Notice the context of the saying in the gospels: Christ spoke, not about "a" mountain, but about "this" mountain, while presumably pointing to a nearby peak. Perhaps he was careful to be so specific in order to avoid confusion with the Jewish proverb.

Christ also spoke about plucking up a sycamore tree by its roots, which certainly has no connection with a Jewish proverb.

Notice also that this saying about moving mountains and trees was given in connection with the actual cursing and dying of a fig tree. The Lord pointed to the very tree as he told his disciples that what he had done they could do also - not only to that tree, but also to that mountain.

Surely there can be no valid doubt that the Lord intended his word to be taken literally. Faith really can move mountains!

---

[14] From an article in the magazine "Impact", issue of July, 1976, pg. 6.

[15] John Albert Bengel, <u>New Testament Word Studies</u>, *Volume One; in loc.*; tr. by CT Lewis and MR Vincent; Kregel Publications, Grand Rapids, Michigan;1971.

CHAPTER SEVEN

THE INGREDIENTS OF FAITH

"Faith" is not some kind of abstract mystery that hardly anyone understands. Nor is it like an ethereal mist - quite impossible to grasp. On the contrary, the basic elements of faith are simple and practical. This chapter builds upon the first by exploring some of the characteristics of triumphant faith...

FAITH IS BASED ON KNOWLEDGE

One day a truculent man approached George Whitefield, stuck out his chin, and announced, "You'll never get me to change my faith!" "Oh?" said Whitefield, "perhaps you will tell me, then, just what you believe?"

"I believe what my church believes!"

"Well, what does your church believe?"

"My church believes what I believe?"

"Well," said Whitefield, exasperated but still trying for a sensible reply, "Will you tell me what you believe?"

The man declared, "We both believe the same thing!" And he strode off.

That man had prejudice, but he did not have faith. What he thought was faith was only naive superstition, a gullible acceptance of what someone had told him. There was no informed understanding in his belief.

True faith is not blind, but is based on two things: knowledge of the Word of God; which leads to knowledge of the Son of God. Always faith is linked either with scripture, or with Christ.

Knowledge Of The Word Of God

The Bible says, "Faith comes by hearing, and hearing by the word of God" (Ro 10:17). Faith comes. It is not already there. It does not just happen. **It comes.** Nor does it come alone, or out of a vacuum. It comes in conjunction with the word of God. Faith and the word are inextricably linked. Faith without the word is mere presumption or naive folly. The word without faith is a dead letter, an empty promise. There are three ways in which faith arises from the word of God -

Faith comes from having the word of God in your head.

There is no substitute for reading and studying your own Bible. There is no substitute for hearing the word of God preached. By hearing the word, reading it, meditating on it, faith comes. The scriptures in many places urge upon us the importance of saturating our minds with the sacred pages.

Thus the very first Psalm describes the man whose "*delight is in the law of the Lord, and on his law he meditates day and night. He is like a tree planted by streams of water, that yields its fruit in its season, and its leaf does not wither.* ***In all that he does, he prospers***" (vs. 2-3).

Paul said that faith comes by hearing, which means that faith cannot exist alone. You cannot say merely, "I have faith!" If you do, then I will ask, "Faith in what? Faith for what?" - because faith must focus on a particular person or promise. So we must listen to learn what are proper objects for faith. But listen to what? Many voices speak in this world and claim our faith!

But if your desire is to use faith to do the will of God, then there is only one source to which you can turn - the Bible. In fact, faith **must** be joined to a promise of God, or it is not faith at all. Christian faith simply cannot exist apart from a word from God. Those who wish to be strong in faith have no choice except to immerse their minds in scripture, making themselves familiar not only with the words of the Bible, but also with the intention behind those words.

Note that mere head knowledge of the Bible, an intellectual understanding of it, will not bring forth mountain-moving faith. You may have a detailed mental grasp of the Bible from cover to cover, and yet be void of faith, or have only a cold and lifeless faith, not able to effect any mighty works.

But if you come to the Bible strongly convinced that it is indeed the Word of God, the living God who cannot lie, and if you read it in the anointing and revelation of the Holy Spirit, then it will become a living book to you. The Holy Spirit takes hold of the Word of God and burns it deep into your heart. Then you will come to an inward conviction of its truth, to that certain knowledge that is **really** faith.

I say it again - you certainly have the **ability** to believe, but before that ability can be transformed into the dynamic power of an all-conquering faith, you must discover the promises of God and his will for your life. Your inward capacity for believing must be supplied with practical material on which to work. That is, faith must have a promise to claim, it must have a conviction to stand upon.

Suppose you are sick. Then you read in God's Word, "I am the Lord that heals you," (Ex 15:26b) and you read those words deeply assured of their truth, with the Holy Spirit scoring them into your soul so that you **know** that God is indeed your Great Physician. Then with a shout of praise and victory faith can leap out and lay hold of that promise and through it find the healing you desire.

The same principle applies to any problem or need that you may be facing: that is, true faith cannot exist apart from knowing a promise of God.

Faith Comes From Having The Word Of God In Your Heart.

Paul was not content to leave the scriptures lying fallow in his head. Having said three times that we need to **hear** the word (that is, get it into our **heads**),[16] he then stressed three times the need to lower it about twelve inches!

> *"But what does it say? The word is near you ... in your **heart** (that is, the word of faith which we preach) ... Believe in your **heart** ... For man believes with his **heart**" (Ro 10:8, 9, 10).*

As you have already learned, merely to read or memorise the promises of God is insufficient. Before the promise can create irresistible faith there must be an act of divine revelation, a revelation that banishes all doubt and uncertainty, a revelation that creates deep inner "knowing" that the promise will certainly be fulfilled in your life.

The word "faith" (Greek, "*pistis*") shows this itself, for it really means firm persuasion, deep assurance, strong conviction, sure confidence.

So he who believes, **knows!**

This revelation may arise out of the anointed preaching of the word of God, or it may come as you earnestly pray over the pages of your Bible, asking God to "enlighten the eyes of your heart, so that you may know" (Ep 1:17-18) what he is truly saying to you. Or it may come to you by a direct act of the Holy Spirit, or in some other way. But come it must, or faith will fail. You must get the word out of your head and into your heart!

A fine illustration of this principle is found in the story of Elisha and his servant (2 Kg 6:11-17). The young man was terrified when he saw the Syrian army completely encircling Dothan, but Elisha

---

[16] The text passage is Ro 10:8-17. In relation to getting the word of God into your head, by hearing it, Paul makes three statements: "The word is near you ... that is, the word of faith that we are proclaiming" (vs. 8); and, "How can they believe in One of whom they have not heard? And how can they hear without someone preaching to them?" (vs. 14); and, "Faith comes from hearing the word, and the word is heard through the message of Christ" (vs. 17).

endeavoured to comfort him: "Fear not, for those who are with us are more than those who are with them!"

At that point the young man had the word of God in his **head**, but it wasn't doing him any good. He was still filled with dread. He needed a revelation of the real truth of what the prophet had said. He needed a touch of divine "illumination"; he needed "a spirit of wisdom and of insight;" he needed "the eyes of his heart to be enlightened;" he needed "to be strengthened in the inner man, to have power to comprehend with all saints" what great resources were available to him; he needed "to be filled with the knowledge of God's will in all spiritual wisdom and understanding" (Ep 1:16-18; 3:16-18; Col 1:9).

So Elisha prayed (always a good way to get a revelation of the word of God): "O Lord, I pray thee, open his eyes that he may see!"

And the Lord opened the eyes of the young man and he **saw**.

He saw that "the mountain was full of chariots and horses of fire around about Elisha." That is, **he saw the spiritual reality that lay behind the promise the prophet had spoken**.

That reality always lies behind God's promise. Perceiving it is what turns a mere intellectual belief into irresistible faith!

If you pray, God will open your spiritual eyes also; the word will get from your **head** into your **heart**. It will then cause faith to come alive, ready for marvellous exploits in the name of the Lord!

But there is still a third step. You may have the word of God in your head and in your heart, but it may still be of little benefit to you unless you also learn that . . .

Faith comes from having the word of God in your mouth.

Paul mentions three times having the word in your **head**, three times having it in your **heart**, and also three times having it in your **mouth**: "But what does it say? The word is near you, on your **lips**... confess with your **lips**...For man...confesses with his **lips** and so is saved" (Ro 10:8, 9, 10).

You must face the fact that there is no substitute for your own personal, spoken confession of the word of God.

That is the point at which the faith of most people fails. They familiarise themselves with the promises of God (getting the word into their heads); they pray over the promise and become passionately convinced of its truth and power (getting the word into their hearts); but they balk at boldly, forcibly, with unwavering authority, **speaking that word** into the teeth of their need. They cannot or will not do as their Master did: **speak** to the storm and tell it to hush, **speak** to the tree and tell it to die, **speak** to the mountain and tell it to move, **speak** to the dead man and tell him to rise. Yet that is the very thing Christ himself commands us to do!

This matter of "confessing the word with your lips" is so important I have devoted an entire chapter to it (Ch 4). So I will say no more about it here, but will move on to another characteristic of faith...

Knowledge Of The Son Of God

Remember that we are discussing now the difference between naive presumption and informed faith. Genuine faith is never unreasonable; it does not act out of ignorance or prejudice; it always has a sound rational base. In fact, we are so made that we cannot possibly believe for something which seems to us to be inherently unreasonable. We may wistfully hope for the unreasonable, we may even energetically pray for it, but we cannot believe for it. Wishing for something and believing for it are not the same thing.

There are two things that provide a rational basis for faith: **the Word of God**, and **the Son of God**.

As we have seen, the scripture says that faith comes from hearing the Word of God. But it also says that faith comes from Jesus: "Look to Jesus, the pioneer and perfecter of our faith" (He 12:2a)... (we are justified) through the faith of Jesus Christ (Ga 2:16, twice; an objective genitive, see the footnote in Chapter One.)

Christ is the Author of faith. Christ is the Finisher of faith.

Apart from him Christian faith is impossible.

John said that "faith is the victory that overcomes the world" (1Jn 5:4). But what kind of faith? He answers that question in the very next verse: "Who is it that overcomes the world but **he who believes that Jesus is the Son of God**" (vs. 5).

What happens to the person who really believes that Jesus is the Son of God?

He at once realises that the birth of Christ was the most stupendous event in history, for this Man is "Immanuel" - "God With Us" (Mt 1:23). Nothing greater has ever happened to the human race.

God has dwelt among us!

And with this fact every human soul has to reckon. If Jesus is the Son of God, then we dare not ignore him, but must hasten to embrace him, and to gain his friendship (compare Mt 5:25-26).

Again, if you believe that Jesus is the Son of God, then you know also that he must be alive today, for death could not possibly hold him (Ac 2:24). And if he is alive, then he can certainly do for us all that he did for people in Bible days!

Knowing that he is the Son of God we know that every word he spoke is true, that his promises are completely reliable, that he has power to perform all that he has spoken.

His promises - of pardon, victory over sin, healing, financial supply, love, joy, and peace, fruitful service, righteousness, success and prosperity, eternal life; those and many others - are all filled with substance when we are persuaded that he who spoke them is the Son of God!

Thus a rational basis is provided for faith.

We are not believing unreasonably, or out of blind superstition.

If Jesus is the Son of God it is unreasonable **not** to believe! In fact, to disbelieve makes God a liar (vs. 10). The Father leaves us no option except to have full and wholehearted faith in all that he has promised us in Christ.

Thus Christ becomes both the **object** of our faith and its **source**.

Without him we could **not** believe; because of him we can do no other **except** believe!

FAITH IS AN INWARD CERTAINTY

I have already mentioned that the Greek word translated "faith" means basically "a firm persuasion", or "a deep assurance".

That is an important idea, because it removes faith from the mystical realm in which it is often placed. People frequently think of faith as a kind of independent entity, mysterious, ethereal, which somehow they must try to catch out of the invisible air.

But faith is fundamentally an inner certainty, created by contact with the word of God, under the inspiration of the Spirit of God, and realised through the Son of God.

Hence we read:

> *"I write to you who believe in the name of the Son of God, that you may know that you have eternal life. And this is the confidence that we have in him, that if we ask anything according to his will he hears us. And if we know that he hears us in whatever we ask, we know that we have obtained the requests we made of him"* (1 Jn 5:13-15).

That is a truly exciting passage.

Three times John uses the word "know" and once the word "confidence", and in this way he defines what it means to believe. Here is faith's inner secret: **an unwavering certainty, an unshakeable confidence.** Faith is not wishing or hoping. Faith has no doubt or uncertainty. Faith is knowledge. Faith knows without a shadow of doubt. Faith cannot accept even the possibility of failure.

When you have faith for something you **know** it is accomplished even before you have any visible evidence that your prayer has been answered. After all, once you have tangible proof that your request was granted you don't need faith for it any more. You need faith only **before** it comes to pass.

But you **do** need faith, real faith. Not wishful thinking. And the ingredient of real faith is calm knowledge.

Hear it again: faith doesn't hope, or guess, or complain, or yearn, or doubt, or wonder: **faith knows!**

Hence scripture says,

"Faith is the substance of things hoped for, the evidence of things not seen" (He 11:1, A.V.)

That is also why Jesus said: "Whatever you desire, when you pray, **believe that you receive it**, and you **will** receive it" (Mk 11:24).

And John repeated the same:

*"If we know that God hears us...we know that we have **already** obtained the requests made of him" (1 Jn 5:15).*

In those three references we are told distinctly that after we pray for something on the basis of a promise of God, we must actually believe that it is **already** ours; only then will it be given to us.

The only evidence you need that you have received what you asked for, is faith. Though you see it not, faith is the evidence of it. Though you feel it not, faith gives substance to it. Your natural senses may have no perception of the desired blessing, yet, knowing that God has heard you, you also "know that you have the petition that you desired of him!"

In the gospel of Matthew there is the story of the woman who received healing when she touched the hem of the Lord's garment (9:20-22).

The record declares that "she said within herself..."

She did not boast of a faith that she did not really have. She confessed her faith **within herself**. What you find yourself saying within yourself is what you really believe. You may say many things to other people, but what you say **within**, in the secrecy of your own heart, that is the real measure of faith.

And what was the faith of this woman? What was this deep inward conviction that filled her heart? It was a strong certainty, a sure knowledge that if she but touched the hem of her Master's garment she would be healed of her complaint.

So faith is knowing for certain that what you ask of God he is both **able** to give you, and **will** give you.

You pray. You believe. But then, in the period of time between believing and receiving, there must be no wavering, there can be no doubting. Instead, there will be joy. Faith is so sure of possession, it will rejoice as though possession has already been obtained.

One of the important keys to reaching this place of inner certainty is deep desire....

FAITH IS AROUSED BY DEEP DESIRE

For many people, faith is ineffective because it is not specific. Their faith is vague, too widely diffused. But faith should be sharply focussed.

I accept, of course, that you do have already a kind of general faith in the love and power of God, and in his grace and goodness. Presumably also you have a general confidence in the veracity and authority of the Bible. That broad faith is quite proper, and it is the ordinary foundation of all our believing.

But when you are faced with a specific **need** - say, for an incurable disease to be healed - then you must develop a specific **faith** for that need, based upon a specific **promise** of God.

A person may have a general faith in God, yet have no faith at all that a particular prayer will be answered.

The first kind of faith says, "God can move mountains"; the second says, "I can move **this** mountain!"

The first says, "All things are possible for God!" The second says, "**This** thing is possible for me!"

The first says, "God healed the sick in Bible days." The second says, "God will heal **me** today."

It is easy to say, "Nothing is too hard for God." It is much more difficult to say, **This thing** is not too hard for God!" It hardly takes any faith at all to say, "God can do anything." But only real faith can say (and mean it), "God will do **this** thing!"

Who would deny that God can work miracles? That is not the point. The point is, will he work **this** miracle that you need right now? And the answer to that question depends on whether you can truly believe that he is able to, and will, give you exactly what you ask for.

How you can you arrive at such certainty?

One of the keys is deep desire.

Christ drew attention to this spiritual law when he said, "Whatever you desire, when you pray believe that you receive it, and you will have it" (Mk 11:24). That text begins with **desire** and concludes with **possession**. In between lies prayer and faith. The sequence is: first **desire**, then **prayer**, then **confidence** that the prayer is already answered, then the **materialisation** of the answer.

But the **foundation** is desire, **deep desire**. This desire provokes fervent prayer; it drives the seeker to search the word of God for a promise; it compels faith to break loose, to claim the promise, and to receive a glorious answer from God.

There are some principles that govern the expression of deep desire in prayer -

Expect To Receive The Actual Thing You Desire

Some people seem to act on the assumption that no matter what they desire God will answer their prayer by giving them something different!

That does sometimes happen (as Paul discovered, 2 Co 12: 8- 10); but the ordinary rule of scripture is that you will get exactly what you ask for, if you ask in faith: "As you believe, so will it be done"..."Ask and you will receive, so that your joy may be full"..."Ask, and it shall be given to you"..."You do not have because you do not ask"..."If you know how to give good gifts to your children (when they ask for them), how much more will your Father who is in heaven give good things to those who ask him!"(Jn 16:23-24; Ja 4:2b; Mt 7:11)

Deep desire creates that expectation. The more profoundly you hunger for your prayer to be exactly answered the more unlikely it will seem to you that God would do otherwise.

Your Desire Must be Specific

The first principle demands the second: you must narrow your desires down to the one thing you **most** want. It is not possible to desire, deeply and successfully, several things at the one time, unless there is a true sympathetic bond between them.

Many people fail in their praying, either because they do not know what they really want, or because they desire things that are antipathetic to each other. If you find that you are wanting several disparate things at the one time, then you should delay prayer until you have sorted out your desires and arrived at the one thing you want above all others.

For example, there are many things I might wish to have - a luxury car, a grand mansion, a private yacht, enough money to be financially independent - but I give no time or prayer to any of those, because the thing I want most of all (success in the ministry God has given me) is not compatible with any of them. I concentrate my energy and faith on this one thing that is my deepest desire.

Again, there are many things I might wish to be - a highly skilled pianist, an astronomer, a mathematician, a top politician - all quite laudable ambitions, but none of them consonant with my deepest ambition, which is to fulfil the purpose that God has ordained for me.

So here is a law of faith that you must face: **it is imperative to discover what you really want before you pray.**

That is more difficult than you might think.

In some areas of life it may take several years for you to discover what you want most of all.

At other times you may delude yourself by covering up your real wants - either because you feel guilty about them, or because they do not reflect what your friends think you should be, or what they expect from you.

Then again, people can desire something on the surface of their lives, while actually choosing its opposite in the depths of their souls. For example, many sick people unsuccessfully pray for healing, because, when all the camouflage is stripped away, they actually prefer to be ill rather than well - perhaps because they need the sympathy their suffering brings them, or because they subconsciously want to punish themselves for some sin, or because they are afraid to face the responsibilities they would have to assume if they were healed.

You will see then, that there is need for strict honesty, to ferret out all the changing wants, wishes, fantasies, and desires that flit in and out of your head, until you finally discover the one thing that represents your true desire.

This rule must be followed in all the issues of life, both those that are most fundamental, affecting your whole life, and those that are more immediate and circumstantial. Find out first what you really want, and then, so long as it is not antagonistic to the purpose of God, pray for that with all confidence. Indeed, once you **have** discovered your true desire, you will probably find it **easy** to pray with complete certainty that God will give you what you ask!

The exception in that last sentence is the next point...

Your Desires Must Conform To God's Will

This matter of deep desire is fundamental. It affects your very being, it determines your destiny.

Solomon taught it: "Keep your heart with all vigilance, for from it flow the springs of life"..."Keep (my words) within your heart, for they are life to him who finds them, and healing to all his flesh." And the Psalmist cried: "Unite my heart to fear thy name." The Apostle also: "If any of you lacks wisdom (or any other promised thing) let him ask God...**but let him ask in faith, with no doubting,** for he who doubts is like a wave of the sea that is driven and tossed by the wind. That person must not suppose that a double-minded man, unstable in all his ways, will receive anything from the Lord" (Pr 4:23, 21-22; Ps 86:11; Ja 1:5-8).

The unstable person, and the waverer; the person who does not know what he wants, or whose heart is torn between two desires; the person whose mind is divided, or who takes no care to guard, guide, control, the inner springs of his being - all of those share one thing in common: **God will not answer their prayers**!

Now such passages show not only that your desires must be specific and stable, if you are to succeed in prayer, but that your desires must also be brought into harmony with God's will.

That means there is one desire that must be for you the chiefest of all, before which all others must yield. One desire must have absolute precedence.

What is it?

Simply this: **"Let thy will be done, O Lord!"**

Plainly, God will not grant any petition that is against his will, or contrary to his nature, or antagonistic to scripture. Therefore, effective prayer will always be submissive to the Father's will.

Christ displayed this submission when he prayed,

> *"My Father, if it is possible, let this cup pass from me; nevertheless, **not as I will but as you will**"* (Mt 26:39).

The Psalmist also, wrote:

> *"**Take delight in the Lord**, and he will give you the desires of your heart"* (Ps 37:4).

God will give you your heart's desire, when you delight in him, because then **your** desire from him will be the same as **his** desire for you.

But now I hasten to add a caution and an admonition. For many people, the declaration "Let thy will be done" is no more than a careless disclaimer of responsibility. They use that expression as an excuse for lazy prayer, for prayer in which there is no faith, for prayer in which they have made no attempt to discover what they themselves truly want, let along what God wants.

That kind of prayer is both futile and inexcusable.

It is true that there are some situations in life (as Christ faced in Gethsemane) when you may be quite unable to discover what God wants you to pray for. You should then do as Christ did - express your personal desire to God, but ultimately surrender the matter to his will.

But in most circumstances it **is** possible to discover whether or not your personal desires are harmonious with God's will. And where it is possible to make that discovery, then you should do so. You will then be able to pray with perfect confidence that what you ask for will be given to you.

There are various ways by which you can discover whether or not it is right for you to exercise faith for a particular thing, and these will be discussed in some detail in other parts of this book. Here I am content to make some general observations...

Your Desires Must Not Violate The Law Of Love

That is, you cannot desire something out of sheer selfishness, nor can you expect God to grant things that will bring wrongful hurt to others.

James tells us that if we desire something simply to consume it on our own lusts then we shall desire in vain (4:3). Whatever we ask in prayer must not be exclusively for our own advantage; some larger benefit must accrue, either to God, or to another person, or to some cause bigger than ourselves.

At the very least (or perhaps I should say the very most) every answer to prayer must bring praise and glory to God. This does not mean that every item of prayer must be a matter of great importance or seriousness. Far from it. You may, and should, pray for quite ordinary, everyday things - even things that are primarily concerned with your personal comfort, satisfaction, and happiness.

But we dare not pray for our own sake alone. In every prayer we should seek to glorify God, and if possible to bring some profit to other people or to the church.

Your Desires Must Be Shaped By God's Word.

But to say that prayer must conform to scripture enlarges the boundaries of prayer almost more than it limits them, for the promises of God are marvellously diverse and rich! So broad is the promise, in fact, that Jesus was able to say "**Whatever** you desire...!"

However, generous though the Lord is, his promise is still conditioned by his will. So John wrote,

*"If we ask anything **according to his will** we know that he will hear us" (1 Jn 5:14-15).*

The corollary must also be inescapably true: if we ask anything against his will he cannot hear us.

The position then is this: if you are a child of God, delighting yourself in him, and if you are confident that you are not asking anything contrary to God's will as revealed in his word, then the scope for prayer is very wide. There are promises concerning pardon, healing, financial supply, strength, comfort, guidance, personal fulfilment, marriage, children, prosperity, success, fruitfulness, peace, joy, necessities of life, home, employment, and many more, embracing virtually every aspect of human life and happiness, and culminating in the resurrection and our inheritance in the kingdom of God.

No wonder Paul said, **"My God will supply every need of yours according to his riches in glory in Christ Jesus."** And again, **"He who did not spare his own Son, but gave him up for us all, will he not also freely give us all things with him?"** (Ph 4:19; Ro 8:31-32).

Your task, and mine, is to discover which of the promises of God is appropriate for our present situation and need, and then build that promise into our spirit until faith blazes out of a passionate desire to see the promise fulfilled. We will then know that God has heard us and that we have the petition we desire of him!

FAITH IS RELEASED BY A POINT OF CONTACT

Faith will not act by itself. It must be released. You must turn your faith loose. You must arouse it, and send it boldly against the mountain that stands in your way. Your faith must be snapped into action.

The Bible often describes how people set a time and a place when they determined that their faith would be activated to produce a miracle.

Here are some examples -

The Israelites claimed the promise of God and marched around the walls of Jericho. Day by day their expectancy mounted, until on the seventh day, in a sudden surge of faith and with all their might, they blew the trumpets loud and long. The enormous impact of thousands of people instantaneously releasing their faith in God shook the walls of Jericho to their very foundations, and with a fearful roar they came crashing to the ground. The city was conquered and Israel rejoiced in God. Faith, released in a specified manner and at a specified time, unlocked God's miracle-working power.

The woman who was healed of the issue of blood said within herself, "If I may but touch his garment I shall be made whole." (Mt 9:21). Closer and closer she drew to the Lord, inch by inch she pressed through the crowd and jostled and pushed until Jesus was just before her. In a fervour of anticipation she reached out her hand and stretched toward him. Nearer and nearer her reaching fingers came to the hem of his garment. In the mighty moving of her faith she shook and trembled until suddenly her longing fingers contacted him. In that moment all of her faith poured forth! It was released between her and Christ, so that healing virtue flowed from the Lord into her diseased body. And in a twinkling she was made whole. She did not expect to be healed when she was twelve inches away from him. But she did expect to be healed the moment she touched him, and that expectancy was a burning conviction deep in her heart. Touching his garment was the point she had set for her faith. It was the point at which she determined to turn loose all of her trust in the healing power of Christ.

Many others had a similar faith, and we read of several occasions when they "brought to him all that were sick, and besought him that they might only touch the fringe of his garment; and as many as touched it were made well" (Mt 14:35- 36; Mk 3:10; etc.).

Later on, when the disciples had taken over the healing ministry of the Lord, Peter's shadow became a point of contact for the faith of people who were sick. It says that "they even carried out the sick into the streets, and laid them on beds and pallets, that as Peter came by at least his shadow might fall on some of them...and they were healed" (Ac 5:15-16). As a sick person lying in the street saw Peter coming towards him, his faith built up to a point of tremendous expectancy, until suddenly, when Peter's shadow touched him, all his believing power burst forth into living contact with God, and he was healed!

In the same way, your faith must be released. It must reach a point of crisis, a moment of irresistible tension, and at that point be turned loose toward the Lord.

That point may be reached by any one of several methods:

>laying on of hands (Mk 16:18)
>
>anointing with oil (Ja 5:14-15)
>
>breaking bread (1 Co 11:28-31; 10:15-16)
>
>gathering two or three believers (Mt 18:19-20)

But whatever your need is, and whatever point of contact you choose, your faith must be released. You must open your heart and let your faith touch the power of God.

Until it is released, faith remains ineffective.

FAITH SEES VICTORY IN EVERY CIRCUMSTANCE

It is said that when Alexander the Great faced the vast Persian army some of his advisers were seized with fear. "What are we against such an immense multitude," they cried. But Alexander retorted, "Is the butcher afraid, though he stands alone before thousands of sheep?" Then another complained, "When the Persian archers loose their shafts, they are so many they obscure the sun!" But Alexander laughed, "It will be more pleasant fighting in the shade!"

I like that! It is small wonder Alexander conquered the world. He faced each conflict, and saw in it only victory. He turned every barrier to his own advantage. He refused to capitulate to fear or doubt. He recognised only the inevitability of his own triumph.

And that is exactly what the scriptures call us to do. Whatever problem or need may be facing us, whatever conflict we may be engaged in, we should calmly declare that we are, and shall be, and can only be, **more than conquerors** through Christ (Ro 8:31, 37).

No army is ever finally defeated until it actually admits defeat and surrenders to the enemy. But such an admission, such a surrender, is unthinkable to the man of faith.

Do you realise that faith can **never** be defeated? Why? Because faith **is victory**! (1 Jn 5:4). Faith is not, and never can be, defeat. It is simply not possible for faith to be overcome.

If we **are** overcome by the world, it indicates only that we have moved away from faith. We may be defeated personally, but **faith** is invincible.

If it appears sometimes that faith has been defeated, then the appearance is deceptive. Either real faith was not present at all; or the apparent defeat is just a stage on the way to a marvellous triumph of answered prayer.

Real faith is victory guaranteed. Real faith is a weapon against which neither this world nor Satan can raise any lasting defence. Faith looks at the world and laughs, exulting in its own strength, turning every situation to the glory of God, seeing victory in every circumstance, knowing that nothing can hinder its ultimate triumph!

FAITH IS RELEASED BY PRAISE

Praise is a proper accompaniment of faith, for faith is more than just an anticipation of victory, **faith is a deep assurance that victory has already been won**. Never once in history has a conquering army been known to sit down howling in despair and fear! Wailing and tears are the mark of those who have lost the battle. Victorious soldiers shout, sing, and rejoice! Likewise, a person who is standing in faith against the world, who knows that victory is already won, should express this confidence in praise. Only as he does this will the victory that is inherent in faith become fully realised in his own life. Those who possess, rejoice in their possessions; so, a possessing faith is inevitably a rejoicing faith.

It is wise to remember that men first began to sin when they stopped praising God (Ro 1:21). Conversely, by the faith that praise releases, and by the strength that praise imparts, we can readily take authority over all the power of the enemy (Lu 10:19-20), and so conquer sin and the world.

CONCLUSION

These things, then, are the characteristics of faith. This is the faith that overcomes the world, the faith that knows no defeat, for it can only be victorious. I have tried to cover in this chapter all of the salient features of this triumphant faith. Now we must embark on a more detailed exploration of this exciting territory, knowing that no matter how far we travel, continents of truth will remain undiscovered - for faith, like love and hope, is one of those eternal virtues that abide for ever, increasing in the endless glory of God.

CHAPTER EIGHT

THE NATURE OF FAITH

The Bible says, "Faith is the assurance of things hoped for the conviction of things not seen... And without faith it is impossible to please God. For whoever would draw near to God must believe that he exists and that he rewards those who seek him" (He 11:1, 6).

That is one of the most important passages in the Bible, for it is the only place where a formal definition of faith is attempted. There are scores of places where faith is demanded, illustrated, applied; but nowhere else is it defined.

Our task in this lesson is to try to understand that definition, and so to provide a sound foundation for all that will follow.

FAITH AND REALITY

Our text declares that faith deals with two different kinds of reality

> things that are future
>
> things that are not seen

Obviously, neither of those areas is susceptible to ordinary discovery. There is no natural faculty (unless faith is defined as a natural faculty) that can either penetrate the future, or grasp what the apostle calls "things not seen" (that is, things that are not part of this natural world.) Only **faith** can capture the future, turning speculation into certainty; only **faith** can reach beyond the physical and grasp the immaterial. Faith seizes tomorrow and makes it bright as today; faith also laughs at natural limitations, and leaps into that spiritual realm where the only reality is God.

The future is real. The things unseen do exist. Both of those areas embrace real facts. But they are such that our ordinary five senses cannot ever discover them. The man who limits himself to what his natural senses can encounter will live all his days sadly impoverished. He will miss the **greater** reality. He will never discover the **first** dimension.

The future is larger than the past or the present; and the things unseen are more tangible, more enduring, than the things that are seen. Yet this greater reality, this first dimension, remains indiscoverable to the wholly natural person, the person who despises faith. For faith, **and faith alone**, has the ability to transcend the **secondary** dimension of time and space, and to grasp those things that belong to the **primary** world, the world of God.

Why is that so? Simply because the natural senses are wholly enclosed within their own limitations. The eye will believe only what it can see; the ear, only what it can hear; the hand, only what it can touch; and so on. Those senses are slaves to themselves, and to each other. But faith is servant of none. It is the master of all senses. Faith calls the senses to its service. It takes hold of the evidence of the senses, and uses this evidence to support its actions, to guide its decisions.

If necessary, faith can even discard all that the eye sees, and the ear hears, or that the hand touches, and leap boldly onto the water of God's promise, walking there in total disregard of natural law. The law of the senses is secondary. The law of faith is primary. That is why the apostle said, "**We walk by faith, not by sight**" (2 Co 5:7)

There is a dreadful transience about everything that belongs to the natural world. There is not one part of it that is not doomed to perish. Those who accept only what their natural senses encounter (unaided by faith), are like passengers embarking on a ship they know will sink, but refusing to have any lifeboats on board. By giving their natural senses top priority, those people are linking themselves to a world that has one appointed end: annihilation. By insisting on believing only what their senses tell them, those people condemn themselves to the obliteration that overtakes all merely material things.

Faith places priority where it belongs: in the world unseen, and in the future appointed by God. As Paul said:

> *"We look not to the things that are seen, but to the things that are unseen; for the things that are seen are transient, but the things that are unseen are eternal" (2 Co 4:18).*

Faith finds its heroes in men like Abraham, who turned his back on the decaying cities of this world, and "looked for the City which has foundations, whose builder and maker is God." Faith sees that the only world with foundations is the world that is future, and unseen. All else is built on quicksand. So faith desires that "better country, that is, a heavenly one" (He 11:10, 13-16).

Let us look more closely at these two areas in which faith operates -

THE FUTURE AND THE UNSEEN

Faith - The Assurance Of Things Hoped For

Are you hoping for some good thing to happen to you? If that hope is grounded in God and his promise, then faith will translate it into a certainty, so real that it will seem to be already accomplished. Faith confirms the inevitability of the things we hope for in God, it is the guarantee that the things we are waiting for will happen. But how does faith do these things?

The Evidential Value Of Faith

The person who has never felt the witness of faith cannot imagine the impact it makes on the believer. Faith has an evidential power of its own that is just as impressive, in fact more so, than the evidential power of the natural senses.

To ask why that witness is so compelling, is as futile as asking why the evidence of the eye is so compelling. The eye sees, tells what it sees, and no one thinks to question the reliability of its witness. What the eye sees is believed.

The same applies to all the natural senses. So long as the conditions are not abnormal, or our faculties are not diseased, or have not for some reason become unreliable, we trust the evidence they bring. Yet (as any reader in philosophy knows) there is no truly rational basis on which we can justify our confidence in those faculties. There is no absolute way in which we can prove that the eye sees what is actually there. Yet we "know" that it does. How do we know? We just know! The eye conveys to the mind its own witness that what it sees is reliable, and the mind is satisfied.

So it is with faith. The man who believes, **knows**. He does not believe because he knows - **he knows because he believes**!

What part then do the natural senses play in the operation of faith?

It is their task to gather what evidence they can, to explore reality to the limit of their ability, and thus to supply faith with information on which to decide whether or not there is scope for it to work. This is the principle expressed by the apostle:

> *"By faith we know that the world was created by the word of God, so that what is seen was made out of things which do not appear" (He 11:3).*

The natural senses tell us that the world exists in the present. But they can never penetrate the veil of the past; they cannot leap back to the beginning, and so discover the origin of all that exists. Yet faith, commencing with the evidence the senses supply, exercises its own faculty, and at once **knows** that by divine fiat alone the seen was created out of the unseen. Faith conveys this certainty to me as surely as the eye conveys the certainty that it sees a rock.

For a man who has never exercised faith to mock the witness faith brings, is inane. It is akin to a blind man mocking those who describe what they see, or to a deaf man mocking those who claim that they hear.

Suppose all the world were blind and deaf, and only a few had eyes and ears. What do you think the attitude of the majority would be to those few when they tried to describe the beauty they could see and the songs they could hear? No doubt the many would greet the few with derisive scorn.

As it happens, the reverse is actually true. The few people in our society who are blind and deaf must believe what the majority says, or else reckon that all men apart from themselves are insane. Yet it must be immensely difficult, if not impossible, for the blind and the deaf to really understand what sight and hearing mean to people who possess those faculties. The fact is, the eye has evidential value only to those who look, and the ear, only to those who listen.

So faith has evidential value only to those who believe. But those who do believe, KNOW!

Faith Cannot Supplant The Senses

It may be thought from the above that I am suggesting that faith is in every way superior to the senses. That would, of course, be a foolish suggestion.

Faith may in some special cases override the evidence of the senses - not so much by countermanding them as by locking into another law, a law higher than that which governs the senses. But in no way can faith replace the senses.

There are some kinds of evidence that only the eye, or the ear, or one of the other faculties can gather. Faith can no more replace the eye than the eye can replace the ear. Each has its proper function. There are tasks for which one or more of our natural senses are wholly adequate. To suppose that faith can displace the senses in those tasks is folly - of which some have been guilty.

The apostle is careful to limit the only two cases in which it is proper for faith to function: faith gives **substance to the things we hope for**; and faith provides **evidence of the things we do not see**. Here then is the difference between the senses and faith. The senses deal with the **present**, and that which is **seen**; faith deals with the **future**, and that which is **unseen**.

We may expand these two areas in which faith operates a little, but only a little. We may expand "future" to include all time that lies beyond sense-knowledge - that is, the past as well as the future - for faith can know all that God has revealed about his activities, from the beginning until the end. And we may expand "unseen" to include the scriptures, for they are seen yet unseen. The hand can hold the Bible, the eye can read it, the ear can hear it, the mind can understand it, yet the reader may still fail to "know" that it is God's word, he may still fail to meet God in the sacred page. Faith alone can transcend the printed lines and transform scripture into a glorious divine revelation, the source of life and power.

Normal And Abnormal Conditions

I said above that the evidence of the senses is fully reliable only when they are free of disease or malfunction, and when the conditions for their use are normal. The same is applicable to faith. Faith operating in an abnormal way, or under false conditions, will give distorted knowledge; its results will not be in harmony with the purpose of God.

The malfunction of one of the natural senses may not be a complete tragedy, but a malfunction of faith can bring irretrievable ruin. This study is an attempt to lay down true guidelines, so that your faith may conform to **the scriptural pattern**. The Bible alone contains reliable instruction about how to believe and receive the promises of God. There is no other source to which we can turn for sound teaching on faith.

This study should do no more than reflect the revelation about faith that God has given us in scripture.

The Assurance Faith Gives

Faith, we have learned, perceives as reality things that have not yet been revealed to the senses.

Nowhere is that more happily true than when faith gives reality to things we hope for. The apostle uses a particular word to describe this result of faith: "*hypostasis*", which means literally, "to give substance to". When faith is linked with hope, faith gives to that hope such vivid confirmation, such concrete form, that it seems to be fulfilled already. Not the slightest possibility exists that our hope will remain unrealised.

What is this hope? How does faith make it substantial?

Our hope is manifold. To begin, there are many sweet blessings God has promised us in Christ that belong to this life, which may not yet be part of our experience, but which we are hoping to appropriate by faith. Then we hope also for all of the sting to be removed from death, and for the grave to hold no power over us. We look for Christ's return and the rapture of the church. We anticipate with awe and excitement the magnificent inheritance God has prepared for us. These promised favours and many more comprise our hope.

Faith gives substance to this hope of ours simply by causing us to know without doubt that the scripture speaks truly, as the very word of God, when it sets this hope before us. The witness is sure. The inner conviction is certain. Faith grasps the scripture, at once recognises the accents of heaven, and conveys this testimony to us that God himself is speaking and his word will surely come to pass!

This is the kind of assurance the apostle talks about when he writes: "When God desired to show more convincingly to the heirs of the promise the unchangeable character of his purpose, he interposed with an oath, so that through two unchangeable things, in which it is impossible that God should prove false, **we who have fled for refuge might have strong encouragement to seize the hope set before us**. We have this as a sure and steadfast anchor of the soul, a hope that enters...where Jesus has gone as a forerunner on our behalf" (He 6:17-20).

Our personal responsibility in this matter is simply to apprise ourselves of what the scripture teaches, to come to a good understanding of the hope God has given us in Christ, and then to plant our faith in that hope. At once faith will cause us to know that what we hope for we have! It is ours now! We but wait with patient confidence for its ultimate realisation.

It should be noted that faith not only brings confirmation that our hope is valid, it is also the vital key to personal fulfilment of that hope. Without faith, the hope remains void of comfort for our souls. But also, without faith, the hope cannot even begin to materialise.

Faith tells me my hope is valid; faith brings my hope to fruition. Hence we are warned against casting faith aside: "Do not throw away your confidence, which has a great reward. For you have need of endurance, so that you may do the will of God and receive what is promised...'My righteous one shall live by faith, and if he shrinks back my soul has no pleasure in him'" (He 10:35-39).

Faith - The Conviction Of Things Not Seen

There are four unseen things of which faith alone can give true knowledge -

God

Some aspects of the knowledge of God are attainable without faith. For example, Paul insists that "ever since the creation of the world (God's) invisible nature, namely, his eternal power and deity, has been clearly perceived in the things that have been made. So (unbelievers) are without excuse; for although they knew God they did not honour him as God" (Ro 1:18-21). Paul claims that the physical creation gives plain knowledge about God, and about his existence and glorious power. Hence, those who deny the existence of God can do so only by wilfully rejecting the witness of their own senses.

The psalmist made the same claim:

> *"The heavens are telling the glory of God; and the firmament proclaims his handiwork. Day to day pours forth speech, and night to night declares knowledge...Their voice goes out through all the earth, and their words to the end of the world" (Ps 19:1- 4).*

However, there are other aspects of the knowledge of God that only faith can discover, and this in two ways: firstly, by believing the revelation God has given of himself in scripture; secondly, by personal encounter with God in life situations - encounters that bring experience of God's love and supernatural strength.

This study is essentially an explanation of how faith encounters God. I am striving to show you how, by faith, and by faith alone, you can better know God and more richly embrace all of his marvellous promises. Apart from faith not even the wisest or most brilliant of men can make such a discovery.

The Spiritual Realm

There is a spiritual dimension that exists parallel to our physical dimension - it is the world inhabited by God, and by his holy angels, and by the demon powers of darkness. This spiritual dimension lies almost completely beyond the apprehension of our natural senses. It becomes apparent to the senses only when it obtrudes into the physical world - that is when angels, or demons, or God himself, choose to become tangibly manifest, to show themselves in visible form, or to act with material resources. Even then, an unspiritual person, a total unbeliever, will probably fail to recognise the true nature of what he is seeing or experiencing.

Basically this spiritual dimension is apprehensible by faith alone, in four ways -

1. Faith discovers its existence, and experiences its reality. Faith brings a vivid perception of the spiritual dimension, so that it becomes eventually more substantial than the physical. The spiritual is seen to be greater, to be eternal, and to have supremacy over the physical in almost every way.

Faith lives with a sparkling awareness of heaven at least equal to its awareness of earth; and with an awareness of eternity at least equal to its awareness of time.

Faith encounters the supernatural as richly as the natural, and the things of the spirit as powerfully as the things of the flesh. The special beauty of this is that faith has access to two worlds (the spiritual and the physical), whereas the senses unaided have access only to one (the physical); but when the senses ally themselves to faith, then they too experience the grace and power of the spiritual world.

2. Faith perceives the influence the spiritual world has on the physical, and recognises the supernatural causes underlying many seemingly natural events.

A classic example is the story of Job. The prologue to Job exposes the spiritual factors that lay behind the succession of disasters that overtook the patriarch and his family. Those spiritual factors (at least at the time) appear to have remained unknown to Job and his friends. But at some later date, a person of faith discerned the real nature of what happened and recorded it for our edification.

So faith recognises the hand of God behind happenings that the ungodly think are mere coincidence, or accidental, or have a natural cause. Faith also identifies the satanic origin of many events - a concept that to an unbeliever may seem to be naive superstition; but to a believer it is fundamental to a life of victory.

3. Faith comprehends, in a way that lies quite beyond the natural senses, the laws and principles that govern the operations of the spiritual world, and it learns how to blend these spiritual laws with physical law, how to unite the natural with the supernatural.

Thus, faith alone is able to recover the unity that God intended should always have obtained between heaven and earth, between time and eternity, and between his realm and ours.

Sin introduced a tragic hiatus between the spiritual and the natural that threw our world into confusion. A dichotomy has been created that was never part of God's original intention. But faith banishes this dichotomy, and produces a fusion of the two worlds into one, so that the man of faith lives harmoniously, alike with both natural law and spiritual law. He is equally at home in both dimensions. He holds them in happy balance, knowing when to depend on the one set of principles or the other, or on both together.

4. Above all, faith encounters the Holy Spirit. Faith perceives his presence in the world, recognises his activity, unites itself to him, draws on his resources, is nourished by his influence, enriched by

his wisdom, invigorated by his touch, directed by his will, emboldened by his example, and inspired by his love.

Conversely, apart from the ministry of the Spirit faith could not exist; for without his enlivening touch faith remains a dead letter, incapable of penetrating the sense barrier, unable to grasp the things of God. Only the presence of the Holy Spirit with you as you study this lesson can transform the head knowledge it will give you about the doctrine of faith into a power of believing that will laugh at all impossibility and rejoice in a mighty experience of answered prayer.

Scripture

There is an aspect of scripture that is seen, and an aspect that may be described as "unseen". The part that is seen is the Bible itself, and any person of reasonable intelligence may read it and understand its contents. Yet, although they may grasp the apparent meaning of what they read, they may completely fail to discover its inner power. For intellectual apprehension, unaided by faith, will never cause scripture to yield its treasures of healing and life.

This is the "unseen" dimension of scripture, a dimension that is accessible to faith alone. True, the eye must read, and the ear must hear before faith can work - "How are men ...to believe in him of whom they have never heard? ...So faith comes from what is heard" (Ro 10:14-17). But unless faith also comes to meet the word of promise, the eye may see and the ear hear all day long without result.

Without faith, the scripture is as ineffectual as a nursery rhyme. Hence we read of some to whom the good news came, just as it has come to us,

"but the message which they heard did not benefit them, **because it did not meet with faith in the hearers**" (He 4:2).

Faith seizes the witness of the eye and of the ear about the contents and veracity of scripture; but then faith realises that there is much more in the sacred page than eye or ear can ever discover. Faith senses the presence of the Spirit of God. Faith recognises that this word is no human invention, that "no prophecy ever came by the impulse of man, but men moved by the Holy Spirit spoke from God" (2 Pe 1:21). Scripture, in fact, will admit its identity as the word of God only when it is challenged by faith. The man who believes the word **knows that it is the word**!

In the face of unbelief the Bible remains a dead letter. The word of God is one area of knowledge that is ultimately discoverable only by faith - no other faculty can expose its true riches. Peter summarises this discovery that faith makes in scripture: "God's divine power has granted to us all things that pertain to life and godliness, through the knowledge of him who called us to his own glory and excellence, by which he has granted to us **his precious and very great promises**, that through these you may escape from the corruption that is in the world because of passion, and become partakers of the divine nature" (2 Pe 1:3- 4).

The Realised Promise

To faith alone belongs the extraordinary honour of giving existence to that which does not yet exist. It sees before the eye sees. It experiences an event before it has happened. Faith grasps the promise of God and reckons it to be already accomplished. Faith is never future, it is always **now**.

As far as faith is concerned, the thing God has promised is already done. Faith accepts the inevitability of the divine law: "whatever you ask in prayer, **believe that you receive it**, and you will"; and again, "if we know that God hears us in whatever we ask **we know that we have obtained the requests made of him**" (Mk 11:24; 1 Jn 5:14-15).

In other words, faith conveys its own witness that prayer has been answered. It needs no evidence other than itself. Faith prays, believes, and at once **receives**. Faith does not wait for an answer; faith reckons itself to be immediately in possession of the answer. Faith gives concrete reality, undeniable substance, to the desired object. To faith, it has already happened.

Notice how Jesus said, "believe that you receive it and you will." Here is a strange mixture of present and future tenses. But the meaning is simply this: the answer to your prayer may be future as far as sense-knowledge is concerned; but to faith it is already a fact. Faith receives immediately. Faith does not wait for tomorrow. Faith sees the answer as happening now.

Faith has no need of any outward materialisation to bolster its confidence; it needs no supporting evidence; it acknowledges nothing more tangible than itself. Faith is satisfied with the promise of God; and having prayed on the strength of that promise, it joyfully believes that it has already obtained a good answer from God.

So faith has the special gift of seeing an object as existing already, although it has not yet materialised. Faith sees now what the eye cannot yet see. Faith holds now what the hand cannot yet touch. Faith perceives now what still lies beyond the perception of the senses.

The senses may say I am still sick, but faith says I am healed. The senses may say I face financial need, but faith says the need is already met. The senses may say that the storm winds are howling, but faith walks in the calm.

Always to faith the promise of God is the only substantial thing; all else is illusory. Faith's bold acclamation is, "Let God be true, and every man a liar" (cp. Ro 3:4).

If faith has to choose between its own evidence, based on the promise of God, and the evidence of the senses, **then faith always chooses in favour of itself.**

So that which the eye cannot see, which the natural man says does not yet exist, faith sees clearly. What God has promised, and faith has appropriated, is at once more real to faith than any other reality. **"Faith is the evidence of things unseen"** - it affirms that what the natural senses cannot perceive, does in fact exist.

The "unseen" becomes "seen" when faith remains firm in its commitment to the promise of God.

CHAPTER NINE

NUGGETS OF FAITH

Sparkling rubies, flashing emeralds, glowing pearls - none of those precious jewels could be any more valuable to you than the gems of faith you will discover in this chapter!

Here, as in the previous chapter, we continue our search among some of the fascinating faith-words that can be found in the New Testament.

MANDATE - "*RHEMA*"

I have shown you that faith, to be effective, must have a **mandate from God** - that is, a specific promise or command, which is applicable to a specific situation.

The Greeks had a word to describe such a divine mandate; it was **"*rhema*"**.

"*Rhema*" occurs many times in the NT. It is used both in a general sense and in a technical sense. In its general use, "*rhema*" means any kind of spoken utterance, and it was a very common word in the Greek world. In its more technical use, "*rhema*" means a particular command, direction, promise, or prophecy, especially when the idea of a **mandate** is present.

A clearer sense of this technical meaning of "*rhema*" may be gained by comparing it with another common Greek word **"*logos*"**. "*Logos*", like "*rhema*", was often used to describe any conversation or utterance, and the two words are frequently interchanged in the New Testament.

But "*Logos*" also had a technical use that does distinguish it from "*rhema*". Whereas "*rhema*" conveys the idea of a vivid, immediate, specific, and (usually) brief utterance, "*logos*" conveys the idea of a more abstract and formal style of speech, an extended discourse, a story, narrative, or report.

"Logos" would be used for a whole language, but *"rhema"* for one saying taken out of that language.

"Logos" would be used to describe the Bible as a whole, but "*rhema*" for a particular verse of scripture.

The wisdom of God in its totality is a "*logos*"; but each promise of salvation, or of deliverance, or of supply is a "*rhema*".

Paul's letter to the Philippians is a *"logos"*, but the promise in 4:19 came to the saints at Philippi (and may also come to us) as a *"rhema"*.

"And my God will meet all your needs according to his glorious riches in Christ Jesus."

The distinction between "*logos*" and "*rhema*" is not absolute, and they often trespass on each other's territory; but the difference does exist, and in some passages it is very apparent.

A Personal Promise From God

As I have said, "*rhema*" has the special sense of a **mandate** - that is, an authority from God to do a certain job, or to believe a certain promise, or to receive a certain gift, or to hold a certain office.

That idea of a mandate is the one that most concerns us here.

It is found, for example, in Lu 3:2-3: *"The mandate (rhema/word) of God came to John... and he went into all the region round about the Jordan, preaching a baptism of repentance."*

Now faith cannot exist, nor function, apart from such a divine mandate. To "step out in faith" without a "*rhema*" from God is to step into presumption and ruin. God is not obliged to respond to any mandate save his own. But if you receive a "*rhema*" from God, as John the Baptist did, and act on it, then success is assured.

This idea of a mandate is so intense in "*rhema*" that it often became **identified** with the thing it **authorised**. Hence it was used not only to express the words spoken **about** some matter, but to describe **the matter itself**.

Thus a "*rhema*", as well as being a particular saying, might also be a certain thing, a transaction, or a business. It is used in that sense in Mt 18:16; Lu 1:37, 38, 65; 2:15; 2 Co 13:1.

Thus "*rhema*" illustrates the close connection that scripture often displays between words and events. In the reckoning of the Bible there is a power in words to objectify themselves. The word becomes the thing - the two cannot be separated.

Let us now look at some of the places where "*rhema*" is used in the New Testament. Remember that I am limiting this discussion to those places where "*rhema*" has the specific meaning of a word from God - a word quickened by the Holy Spirit, one that comes to us in the form of a divine mandate. Such a rhema is the only proper basis for faith - to base faith upon any other source is presumption, if not folly.

God Creates By A "*Rhema*"

> *"The world was created by the rhema of God... he upholds all things by the rhema of his power" (He 11:3, 1:3).*

The rhema of God is the word he speaks to a particular situation.

He spoke into nothing and called into existence the entire universe. And now, by the power of that same irresistible rhema, he upholds the heavens and the earth and controls all that happens within them.

God speaks into every new situation, and thus orders the events of each day according to his will. Nothing can ever deny fulfilment to the divine *rhema*.

What God says is done!

The word translated "uphold" is "*phero*", which means to bring, lead, move. Thus we learn that simply by the force of his *rhema*

God compels each new day, each new situation, to fall into conformity with his will.

Likewise, in the life of faith, as we face each new problem or circumstance, our first task is to receive a *rhema* from God applicable to that need. To act without such a *rhema* is to invite disaster. But if you first receive a *rhema*, a mandate from God, then believe it, and then act on it, success is assured. God's *rhema* has creative power.

Mary, the mother of Jesus, vividly expressed this thought in her exchange with Gabriel. The archangel had promised that she would give birth to Jesus through a supernatural conception; then he encouraged her faith by saying, "With God nothing will be impossible." But the word "nothing" is actually "no *rhema*". Mary was being challenged to accept the special promise God was giving her, and by her faith to turn that promise into a living child. Did she or did she not believe that God's *rhema* could never fail? Would she or would she not accept that *rhema* as a personal mandate to her? She proved her faith when she said: "Let it be done to me according to your *rhema*!" (Lu 1:37, 38). And it was done! The word became the thing when that word was spoken in faith.

That is the kind of faith response God is seeking from you and me. To see that nothing is impossible with God; to see that everything God does is achieved simply by a *rhema*; to see that the *rhema* of God can never be defeated; to see that a *rhema* is so closely identified with the thing it describes that possession by faith of the *rhema* will lead inevitably to possession of what the *rhema* promises; to obtain a *rhema* apt for your present need; to believe that *rhema* and to confess it boldly - **that is miracle-working faith!**

Notice again that the Greek text says, "No *rhema* of God is impossible", but the translators have correctly rendered it, "With God **nothing** will be impossible. The "*rhema*", the word of God about the event, is identified with the event itself.

God's word is not insubstantial, ephemeral, a mere vibration of air. The *rhema* of God is so solid, so definite, so utterly sure, that it may be reckoned as already fulfilled! Anyone who has a divine *rhema* can boldly say that those things that are not, already are (Ro 4:17; He 11:1). The *rhema* becomes, indeed is, the thing it describes, for there is no reality, no existence of anything, apart from God's *rhema.* Remember: "*he upholds **all things** by the rhema of his power*" (He 11:3).

This merging of God's word into the thing it describes is also seen in Lu 2:15: "*The shepherds said to one another, `Let us go over to Bethlehem and see this **thing** (rhema) that has happened!*'" Used in that manner, *rhema* displays a deep recognition that behind everything God does stands his word. You can't have a happening without a *rhema*; and you can't have a *rhema* without a happening! The word is the thing itself. If you have the word, then you have the event it promises.

The ultimate reality, therefore, is God's word. Hence true faith never measures the word by reality, but always measures reality by the word. If God has said it, that settles it! The word will supplant all other reality, especially when that word is believed and acted on.

Here is another intriguing passage: "*We are witnesses to **these things** (rhemata), and so is the Holy Spirit whom God has given to those who obey him*" (Ac 5:32). The "things" were all fulfilled *rhemata* - events that happened in obedience to the voice of divine prophecy, command, or declaration. The event and the word were so inextricably intertwined that the one could always be described in terms of the other. The same principle is applicable today.

The *Rhema* Is Life

> "*Man shall not live by bread alone, but by every rhema that proceeds from the mouth of God*" (Mt 4:4)

Here again is this sense of a divine mandate; of God's *rhema* commanding, and at the same time giving the believer strength to obey; of authorising, and at the same time equipping with power; of promising, and at the same time conveying faith for its fulfilment.

Just as we need daily bread to sustain physical life, so we need a daily *rhema* to sustain spiritual life. In fact Christ intimates that the latter is more needful than the former. Possessing the former alone, a man may die twice and be forever cut off from God. But with the latter, a believer possesses inviolable life in every part of his being - nothing can touch him save what that *rhema* permits.

So the source of real life is a *rhema* from God. A sinner receives a *rhema* and at once knows his sin is forgiven. A defeated person receives a *rhema*, and grasps a new and glorious victory. A sick person receives a *rhema*, and health floods into his being. A *rhema* turns failure into success, despair into joy, poverty into plenty, and perplexity into wisdom.

Wherever "death" has touched you, in spirit, mind, or body, seek a *rhema* from God - your own personal mandate to live abundantly and to be whole. If you can get such a word, and then believe it, and act on it, the devil will have to leave you as he left Jesus, and you will be ministered to by the angels of God! (vs. 11).

The Irreversible Word

The word of God is always irresistible and it will always fulfil itself in the way God has appointed.

Sometimes divine decree makes human faith the key to releasing that word; other times the word will fulfil itself independently of human response.

One graphic example of that principle is seen in Christ's prediction that Peter would betray him. Christ spoke a *rhema*: *"Then he (Peter) began to invoke a curse on himself and to swear, `I do not know the man.' And immediately the cock crowed. And Peter remembered the saying (rhema) of Jesus, "Before the cock crows,* *you will deny me three times." And he went out and wept bitterly"* (Mt 26:74-75).

Remember the *rhema*! When God speaks, don't forget it! Perhaps God's *rhema* to you will lie dead, because it requires a faith response that you refuse to give it. Yet you may one day be asked to account for your failure to realise that precious mandate.

However, there are times when God may speak to you about your life in terms that are independent of faith. You can be sure that his saying will come to pass. No word of God is void of power. Peter tried to deny that particular *rhema* of Christ; he insisted that it would not, could not, eventuate. But happen it did, exactly as the Lord had said.

It is to be hoped that the fulfilment of his word to you will lead, not to bitter tears, but to inexpressible joy. In any case, his word cannot be reversed.

Act On The Word Alone

In this part of our study of *Faith Dynamics* I am trying to stress how absolutely necessary it is for you to obtain a personal word from God - one that applies to your particular need. Real faith can flourish only on the foundation of such a word.

The technical name for that word, or promise, is *rhema"* - which means a special mandate from God that comes directly to you, and which authorizes you to believe for a certain benefit, or to follow a certain course of action.

Once you have received from God such a *rhema*, it alone should govern your actions. To act without it is presumption; to fail to act once you have it is unbelief. A *rhema* gives you the right to act in faith, no matter how impossible the circumstances may seem to be. You cannot fail if you act on the basis of the mandate God himself has given you.

Peter discovered that exciting fact when he went fishing with the Lord. For many weary hours the disciples had scoured Galilee and caught nothing. But now, at a time of day considered to be poor for fishing, Jesus commanded them, "*Put out into the deep and let down your nets for a catch.*" But Peter answered, "*Master, we toiled all night and took nothing! Yet at your **word** (rhema) I will let down the nets.*" And when the disciples did this they enclosed a great shoal of fish, so numerous the two boats were filled to sinking point! (Lu 5:4-11)

The trigger for that miracle was a man who said, "The situation is hopeless; **but I will still act according to the *rhema* Christ has given me!**"

The *rhema* Christ speaks cannot fail, nor can those who believe it. Whatever the Lord says to you has power to fulfil itself abundantly in your life! You must measure the *rhema* by itself, **not by your circumstances**. Let the word of the Lord, not the sight of your natural eye, rule your confession and determine your actions.

No wonder Jesus was able to say: "*If you abide in me, and my **words** (rhemata) abide in you, you can ask whatever you will and it shall be done for you!*" (Jn 15:7). The secret of answered prayer is to pray **in response to a divine rhema**. You can't go wrong! The Lord cannot refuse to honor his own word!

You may be wondering how to get a *rhema*?

Jesus answers: "*Abide in me.*" Live in close fellowship with Christ, meditate often in the scriptures, sit under the ministry of God's word, and learn to recognise the voice of God when he speaks.

You should also ask the Lord to give you a *rhema* for your situation. Perhaps it will come to you as a verse of scripture, or through a prophetic utterance, or out of a sermon, or by the advice of a wise friend, or through the deep inner witness of the Spirit. Wait for that word. Don't hurry. With simple trust expect it to come. But when it comes, seize it boldly, confess it confidently, and act on it vigorously!

Christ said to his disciples, "*The words (rhemata) I have spoken to you are spirit and life!*" (Jn 6:63).

How true that is! Any *rhema* of Christ is alive with the power of the Holy Spirit, able to bring life where there is none, and to effect a mighty miracle of answered prayer. If man or devil should seek to entice you away from dependency on that *rhema*, let your reply be the same as Peter's: "Where else shall I go? Christ alone has the words (*rhemata*) of eternal life!" (vs. 68).

Every saying of Christ is alive with power, dynamic with strength. In comparison with his words all other sayings have in them an echo of death.

The *Rhema* Saves, The *Logos* Judges

Here is a thought-provoking passage:

> *If anyone hears my sayings (rhemata) and does not keep them, I do not judge him; for I did not some to judge the world but to save the world... (but) the word (logos) that I have spoken will be his judge on the last day" (Jn 12:47-48).*

Note how Christ draws a contrast between his "sayings" and his "word".

The point of the contrast is this: Jesus did not come to condemn the world, but to save it, and he does this by offering a life-giving mandate (his "sayings"/*rhemata*) to all who receive his doctrine (his "word"/*logos*). But if any man fails to respond to his "sayings", then the "word" will condemn him on the last day.

The *rhemata* save; the *logos* judges!

We may say, then, that

- the ***logos*** (his "word") means the total message of the gospel; including not only its offer of eternal life, but also its revelation of the righteous commandments of God, and its assertion of the coming day of resurrection and of judgment. The *logos* is the full body of doctrine God has given us in scripture, and this entire *logos* will be the law against which every human life will be ultimately measured. This *logos* appeals to our reason, it demands our assent, it requires our allegiance; but it is too vast to be itself the immediate agent of salvation. Some of God's humbler people never reach a real understanding of it. If salvation came only by embracing all that the *logos* signifies then hardly any one could be saved! The *logos* is the final standard of truth; but it cannot be the actual instrument of salvation. That privilege is reserved for the *rhemata*.

- the **rhemata** (his "sayings") are the various promises, exhortations, and instructions of Christ, found in scripture, and designed to provoke faith and obedience, which leads to eternal life.

The *logos* gives instruction in the way of the Lord, exposing his holiness, revealing man's sinfulness, explaining the nature of salvation, and demanding acceptance of its doctrines.

But a *rhema* is a single word of promise, brought to your special attention by the Holy Spirit, inspiring faith, and becoming the door through which you step into salvation.

One *rhema*, if you embrace it with eager faith, is enough to give you access to all of the blessing contained in the *logos*, and to isolate you from its judgment. But failure to respond to that *rhema* may deprive you of the salvation promised in the *logos* and so expose you to all of its penalties.

The *logos* impersonally offers salvation to all men; but a *rhema* is the voice of God, through scripture and the Holy Spirit, speaking to you urgently, intensely, personally, giving you an invitation to believe and be made whole.

Now that is how *rhema* and *logos* may be applied to the vital issue of salvation. But what is true of that most important of all God's promises is also true of the lesser benefits contained in the gospel.

Take, for example, bodily healing. The *logos* contains a complex doctrine of divine healing - some aspects of which are explained in other parts of this course. But it is not likely that you would find healing merely by reading those chapters, or even by studying everything that the Bible teaches about healing. Far more probably, the Holy Spirit would pluck one statement out of the Bible, or out of one of these chapters, or one truth that a lesson contains, or one verse of scripture, and quicken that promise to you so that your faith is aroused for a miracle.

This book is a *logos*; the single promise you might find here is a *rhema*. The Bible is **the** *logos;* the single promise you *might* find there, made alive by the Holy Spirit, is a *rhema*. The *rhema* is the real source of faith, the key to the miracle you need - although the *logos* must remain the basic soil out of which the *rhema* springs. No true *rhema* will ever be contrary to the sound doctrine found in the *logos* (that is, the Bible).

The *Rhema* Must Be Spoken

Paul refers to this matter of a *rhema* being the actual instrument of our salvation (and hence of every blessing contained in that salvation): *"The 'rhema' is near you, on your lips and in your heart (that is, the 'rhema' of faith which we preach)... So faith comes from what is heard, and what is heard comes from a 'rhema' of Christ"* (Ro 10:8,17).

Hearing a *rhema* is the thing that creates faith! But then, **believing** that *rhema* in your heart, and **confessing** it with your lips is the thing that creates salvation (and all of its attendant blessings of healing, strength and supply) in your life.

For you, if you can receive it, believe it, confess it, act on it, God's *rhema* to you is the agent by which all that he desires for your life will be splendidly and delightfully realised.

"Take the sword of the Spirit, which is the 'rhema' of God" (Ep 6:17), and you will find yourself strong in faith, able to quench all the fiery darts of the evil one, and to live triumphantly, enriched by every resource the grace of God can give you!

Before leaving this section, perhaps I should mention again that *rhema* and *logos* do not always reflect the distinctions I have been emphasising. Both words are frequently interchanged in the New Testament and their inner meaning is often blurred. But in their fundamental significance a difference between them does exist, and this difference is high-lighted in passages like those quoted above.

FULLY SUFFICIENT - "*AUTARKEIA*"

Autarkeia occurs three times in the New Testament (once as a verb). It means literally **"self-sufficient"** - not in the rather negative sense that the phrase commonly has, but in a favourable sense. It conveys a vivid picture of total adequacy for every situation - an adequacy we possess already in Christ, but one that must be released by a faith-confession.

Here are the three places where the word occurs -

> *"God is able to cause all grace to abound toward you, in order that in everything you may always have all self-sufficiency, so that you may abound in every good work"* (2 Co 9:8)

> *"Not that I speak according to lack; for I have learned, in whatever position I find myself, to be self-sufficient"* (Ph. 4:11)

> *"There is great gain in godliness with self-sufficiency"* (1 Ti 6:6).

You Have Everything You Need

Because "self-sufficient" can have an unfavorable sense in English, using that expression as a translation of *autarkeia* poses some risks. So translators tend to adopt a softer rendering, based on a secondary meaning of *autarkeia* - namely, "contentment". Hence the KJV reads: "I have learned, in whatsoever state I am, therewith to be content." But to make Paul say only that he was "contented" quite fails to convey the vitality of the Greek.

Perhaps a good idea of the real significance of *autarkeia* can be gained by comparing it with an English derivative. In commercial life, the word "autarchy" is used to describe a condition of economic self-sufficiency; it refers to a country or community that is able to prosper without dependence on imports from other places. The people have everything they need in their own land to sustain good health and happiness. An "autarchy" lacks nothing that is essential to build national prosperity and strength.

In Christian life, the term "autarchy" would describe that place God has created for us in Christ, in which we can stand by faith, and where we find within ourselves the capacity to cope with any situation. Living in union with Christ we possess enough resources to meet any demand, sufficient strength to overcome every foe. We are independent of outside assistance, unaffected by external circumstances, competent to handle whatever life brings before us.

Now that gives to *autarkeia* a much more vigorous meaning than mere "contentment". Those who have discovered *autarkeia* in Christ cannot just sit down, placidly passive, letting life do to them what it will. Rather, *autarkeia* expresses a frame of mind in which we confront every situation with boldness, knowing that every internal and external enemy has been defeated, that the grip of poverty has been broken, that God has made us rich, so rich that we can affirm as extravagantly as Paul does: ***"in everything I am always fully self-sufficient so that I can abound in every good work God sets before me!"***

The essence of *autarkeia* is that God has already given us in Christ all that we need to triumph over every adversity. We are his new creation, complete in Christ, refashioned after his likeness, possessing amazing resources that are more than sufficient for every challenge we may face.

Such a person will no doubt be content; but hardly content to be nothing more than content!

However, it is one thing to possess these resources, it is another to live in the enjoyment of them. The outworking of this *autarkeia* depends on three things -

1. We are wholly indebted to Christ for our sufficiency. From ourselves, before we met Christ, we could have expected nothing but poverty, defeat, and death in isolation from God.

So whatever we now have is of God, his gift to us in Christ, and can be no source of personal pride, but only of gratitude and praise.

2. However, now that we **have** met Christ, and now that he has made us a new creation so that the old things have passed away and everything has become new, we **are** expected to look at ourselves in a new way.

You should no longer regard yourself from a human point of view, but rather resolve to see yourself as God sees you. You should think about yourself, talk about yourself, as the new person God has made you to be, a person **complete in Christ** (2 Co 5:16-17; Col 2:9-10). God has wrought in you such a perfect work that you can (and should) develop a wonderful new image of yourself.

Many Christians, out of an unfortunate and false sense of piety, refuse to think of themselves as anything other than miserable sinners - weak, defeated, worthless. Christ, to them, is not an integral part of their being, the heart and soul of their life; he is only a kind of God-given camouflage, a heavenly disguise, a spiritual crutch, always external to them. They do not identify themselves with him. They think of him as someone **over there**, strong, good, ever willing to help; meanwhile, they are **here**, still ruined and soiled, desperately hoping that he will come to them, to sustain them in their weakness, to cover their deficiencies, to prop them up when they are under pressure.

For them to say, **"I am self-sufficient,"** or even to think it, seems like obscene blasphemy. Such a thought sears their minds with shame, such a word chokes in their mouths like vomit.

Yet *autarkeia* expresses the image scripture bids me to have of myself. I am to look on myself as so fully integrated with Christ, and Christ with me, that all of his strength, wisdom, ability, and sufficiency are mine. **He is in me, the hope of glory!** (Col 1:27). All of his resources are mine **now**! There is nothing for which I am not adequate - except sin and violation of God's will!

I can assuredly say with Paul, "I am **self-sufficient**," because the "self" I am talking about is the new man Christ has formed!

This brings me now to the third thing on which the outworking of *autarkeia* depends -

3. The practice of a right confession is vital. Listen again to Paul's bold speech: "I am not going to speak about any kinds of lack; for I have learned that no matter what conditions I face I am self-sufficient!"

There is a man choosing to make the right kind of **confession**. He refuses to look at things from a natural viewpoint - if he did, he might well discover many things lacking, and he might be tempted to confess those things, which would surely reinforce his poverty.

He could have said, "I lack money" - but he chose to say, ***"My God will supply every need!"***

He could have said, "Sin is too strong for me" - but he chose to say, ***"I am the righteousness of God in Christ!"***

He could have said, "Disease is at work in my flesh" - but he chose to say, ***"By his stripes I am healed!"***

He could have said, "I can't overcome this habit" - but he chose to say, ***"I am more than a conqueror through Christ!"***

He could have said, "Fear is destroying my life" - but he chose to say, ***"Since God is for me, who can be against me!"***

He may have lacked many things - health, holiness, peace, joy, victory, money, strength, hope, even faith - but he refused to say a word about what he lacked. **Instead, he chose to look at himself** and his circumstances from God's viewpoint, and to confess only what was true of him in Christ.

For the man who takes that stance only one confession is possible: *"I can do all things in him who strengthens me!"* (Ph 4:13). Which is just another way of saying: "This new man Christ has made is **self-sufficient!**"

Always Abounding In All Things!"

The RSV (along with many other translations) gives a rather poor rendering of Ph 4:11. It reads:

"Not that I complain of want; for I have learned, in whatever state I am, to be content."

That is too passive. It lacks the boldness of the original. It fails to convey the sense of a vibrant faith confession. It tends to present a false picture of Paul sighing, "Well, you know that I have many things to complain about - for I have suffered much privation - but I will not complain; for I have learned to accept every situation with patience and contentment - I submit to whatever life brings."

Now that may be a stoic and seemingly pious attitude, and it may be admired by many people, but it does not do justice to Paul. He did not merely refrain from complaint, or just bravely endure whatever came. Rather, he expressed bold self-assurance, dynamic spiritual authority, and a vigorous confession of faith that made him master of every condition. "Whatever condition" he found himself in (from a natural viewpoint) **he knew that he had in himself, as a new creation in Christ, incredible resources of wisdom, strength, faith, and life.**

Nor was this possession of *autarkeia* a prerogative unique to an apostle. Paul certainly spoke out of his own experience; but he also declared that the same grace is given to all of God's people. See the number of times he heaps together the superlative "all" in an attempt to impress on the Corinthians the extravagance of God's gift to them in Christ -

> *"And God is able to cause to **abound** toward you **all** grace, in order that in **all** things **always** having **all** self- sufficiency you may abound to **all** good works!" (2 Co 9:8)*

If your life is joined to the life of Christ, then you too **"always have all self-sufficiency,"** no matter what your conditions may be!

But this grace of God will bring you no benefit unless you gladly embrace it, and boldly confess it. Refuse to be ruled by natural wisdom. Do not speak according to what your eye sees, but according to **what God says**. Not tomorrow, but today, in Christ you fully possess this exciting attribute of *autarkeia*. Since you possess it, confess it - then you will experience it!

Learning The Lesson Of Faith

Notice, Paul said that he had **"learned"** to make this faith-confession; he had **"learned"** how to live out his "self- sufficiency" in Christ. How did he learn? I suppose in the same way we do: by divine revelation, and by hard experience!

But the result of that learning was a deep resolve

- never to talk about his lack, but always about his sufficiency.
- never to acknowledge weakness, but always to profess strength.
- never to see himself from a human viewpoint, but always as God saw him.
- never to think of himself as defeated, but always as victorious.
- never to accept failure, but always to affirm success.

I suppose also that keeping this resolution was no easier for Paul than it is for you or for me. "Learning" for him required the same self-discipline and diligent application that it demands from your and me.

So you must first decide what kind of image you are going to have of yourself - **God's, or your own.** You must decide what kind of confession you are going to make - **according to natural observation or divine revelation.**

Then, when you have decided to see yourself as God sees you, and to say about yourself what God says, you must "learn" steadfastly to maintain this godly image and godly confession.

Satan, the flesh, your natural mind, will all conspire against you. **But hold fast with all your might to your confession of faith.** That confession promises a great reward! That is why Paul wrote to Timothy: **"There is great gain for those who grasp their self-sufficiency, and by it produce godliness."**

May the Christ who is in you teach **you** how to do just that.

CHAPTER TEN

MORE NUGGETS

Search the following pages and you will find more fascinating faith-words that can lead you to the treasures of Christ. This chapter continues on from the last, which dealt with ***rhema*** and ***autarkeia***. The third "nugget" is ....

"MY GLORY" - "*KABOD*"

The Hebrew word *kabod* occurs many times in the OT, with its usual meaning of "glory" or "splendour". But there are a few places where it is found in an unusual setting, in which it appears to refer to the human voice -

> *"Therefore my heart is glad and **my glory** rejoices" (Ps 16:9).*
>
> *"Thou hast girded me with gladness that **my glory** may praise thee and not be silent. O Lord my God, I will give thanks to thee for ever"* (Ps 30:12).
>
> *"I will sing and make melody! Awake, **my glory**! Awake, O harp and lyre!" (Ps 57:8).*
>
> *"But the king shall rejoice in God; all who swear by him shall **glory**" (Ps 63:11).*
>
> *"I will sing and make melody! Awake, **my glory** ... I will give thanks to thee, O Lord, among the nations (Ps 108: 1,3).*
>
> *"Let the saints be joyful in (their) **glory**; let them sing for joy on their couches" (Ps 149:5).*

In each of those verses, "glory" seems to be a description of the human voice, particularly when it is lifted up in praise to God : "my glory rejoices ... my glory will praise thee, and not be silent ... awake, my glory!"

If that is so, then the ancient Hebrews have captured in a most striking way two important ideas

> 1. they have vividly portrayed the idea that man discovers his ultimate dignity, his highest purpose, in the act of worship. This, above all else, is the behavior that separates man from the animal creation. If man does not worship he has lost the essential attribute of his humanity and he becomes little better than the beasts of the field. If he has not spoken in worship he has scarcely spoken at all, for the faculty of speech fulfils its noblest purpose through offering praise to God. Worship is man's **glory**.
>
> 2. they have vividly portrayed the idea that the **human voice itself** is the glory of man, the chief expression in man of the divine image. Beside God, **only man can speak**!

When I talk I display the fact that God has made me in his image!

How shameful for a man to debase this "glory" by uttering foul obscenities, or by polluting his lips with blasphemy, lies, slander, or any other verbal iniquity. How sad to hear him denying this "glory" by speaking words of unbelief, or of fear or rebellion against God.

This "glory" of ours may become our deepest shame and the source of our greater ruin!

Indeed, it is our "glory" only when we discipline our tongues to speak words of faith, worship, and praise.

"Awake, my glory!" the psalmist cried. He wished to stir his tongue into a holy endeavor. He wished to arouse the godly creative power latent in his voice. He wished to speak words that would give him bold access into the presence of God, words that would unlock miracles, words that would mark him as a son of God with power!

Is your voice your glory or your shame? Does it ennoble you or debase you? Does it enable you or debilitate you? Does your tongue dig a grave for you, or does it attract to you the life of God?

Are your words an echo of the divine, or of the demonic?

The psalmist insisted that he would not allow his "glory" to be silent. He was determined to gather together all the vocal resources he had at his command, and to compel every word to speak favorably of God. No word of distrust, nor of unbelief, nor any evil word, would govern his lips. His voice would be under God's control, speaking words that could not be censured, words that would release into his life all of the treasures of the Almighty.

Every soul who speaks thus will find indeed that his voice is his **glory**, and the key to the limitless promises of God!

THE TRIAL OF FAITH - "*DOKIMION*"

Dokimion is used only twice in the New Testament, but it contains an important statement about the nature of faith -

> *"You should fully understand that the proving and testing of your faith will produce patient steadfastness. And let this steadfastness have its full effect, doing a thorough work, so that you may be all that you should be, perfect, complete in all things, lacking in nothing" (Ja 1:3,4; expanded).*

> *"You may have to suffer various trials and temptations, so that your faith may be proved and tested. Thus your faith (much more precious than the perishable gold which is also tested by fire) will redound to your praise and glory and honor at the revelation of Jesus Christ" (1 Pe 1:6-7; expanded).*

Both of those verses stress the need for faith to be tested before it can be approved. Without that fiery trial doubt will always remain, whether or not faith is the genuine article. Perhaps it is fool's gold? The fire will prove it!

The idea behind *dokimion* is drawn from metallurgical chemistry. The picture is one of a piece of metal being melted down in a crucible to test its genuineness and to remove any impurities. Until the metal is submitted to this process it remains a comparatively worthless piece of ore.

So faith must be perfected and purified under trial, until it is approved by God and by the results it obtains. The outward nature of this trial will depend on the kind of faith being tested - whether saving faith, healing faith, financial faith, and so on. Perhaps your faith in Christ as Saviour will be tested in the crucible of persecution; or your faith in the Great Physician may be tried under pressure of pain; or you may be tempted to denounce the goodness of God in the face of personal tragedy or desperate financial need. But underneath the surface conditions every trial of faith consists of two things -

> 1. a delay in the answer to your prayer beyond the point where delay seems to be reasonable. Most people are prepared to accept some delay in the answer to their prayer; but there is a cut-off point, a point beyond which it seems that further delay is intolerable. That is when the trial of faith really begins. If your faith remains firm and unwavering through prolonged delay then it will be stamped *dokimion* - "tested and approved!"

> 2. an assessment of whether your believing is controlled by "sense-knowledge", or by the Spirit-quickened word of God. How much does the divine promise mean to you? How real is it? Can you hold to that word against all the evidence of your natural senses? Which will prevail: the reasoning of your natural mind, or the revealed wisdom of God?

Artificial faith, or faith that is ill-grounded in the word of God, that lacks a Spirit-quickened promise, will eventually collapse under pressure. But approved faith, inspired by the Holy Spirit, undergirded by a word from God (*rhema*), will emerge from the burning crucible all the stronger, purer, more victorious for its time of fierce trial.

Faith that has been "proved" (*dokimion)*, said James, produces **"steadfastness"**; that is, an ability to stand firm in every circumstance, abounding in confidence, able to face the future in the unyielding strength of God. And the result of such steadfastness? It will clear the way for faith to flourish even more richly, so that the believer is able to embrace more and more of God's promise, so that he is complete in all things, lacking in nothing!

Here then is faith, in ever greater measure, possessing the treasures of God; here is faith obtaining everything God has promised; here is faith perfected because it has been proved.

So the "trial" (***dokimion***) is not something to be shunned, but to be embraced with joy. If you attempt to believe God, then you can expect to face this "trial". You cannot truly claim to have faith unless you can hold it under pressure. The only faith you really have is the faith that emerges unscathed, pure and vigorous, from the time of testing.

WORKS - "*ERGA*"

> *"What does it profit, my brethren, if a man says he has faith but does not have works? Can his faith save him? ... So faith by itself, if it has no works, is dead ... Faith apart from works is barren. Was not Abraham our father justified by works, when he offered his son Isaac upon the altar? You see that faith was working along with his works, and faith was completed by works ... You see that a man is justified by works and not by faith alone ... For as the body apart from the spirit is dead, so faith apart from works is dead" (Ja 2:14-24).*

It must be realised that James is not talking about gaining salvation by works, nor about creating faith by works. The person he describes is already a believer, he is already saved. But James asserts that his salvation will wither away, his faith will decay, unless it is matched by corresponding action. Faith acts! Faith is never merely passive. Action is the very spirit of faith.

Without the works that are proper to it faith becomes an empty husk, a dead body, a barren field.

James applies this principle of matching works particularly to the matter of justification (vs 24); but it is applicable to **every** use of faith.

That is shown by his use of Abraham as an illustration. Abraham believed that God was able to raise the dead, and he **acted** on that faith when he laid Isaac on the altar and prepared to sacrifice him. God had already told Abraham that he and Isaac would **both** return from the mountain alive. Abraham believed God. He affirmed God's word, professing confidence that God would do everything he had promised (Ge 22:1-2, 5).

All of the stages of faith are apparent to this point

- a Spirit-quickened word from God, that Abraham would be the father of many nations
- inner belief in that word and surrender to it
- bold confession of that word
- faith tested when the promise of a son was long delayed, and then tested even more severely when he was told to sacrifice Isaac.

But although Abraham had remained faithfull to this point, faith was still not perfected in him. One more trial remained, the trial of **action**. He had to put matching works alongside his words. In Abraham's case, that required holding the knife above his son with every intention of plunging it into the lad's breast.

Thus Abraham proved himself equal to faith's demand. His works matched his faith. He gained an immediate response from heaven.

That is why James argues that faith, by itself, **without actions that properly correspond to it**, is lifeless. No salvation can spring from it. No miracle can happen. No fruit can be produced. Faith **works** only with **works**! Without works, faith is incomplete, a cold corpse!

Quoting Abraham again, James asserted that **"faith was working along with his works, and faith was completed by works"**. "Completed" has the sense of being fully discharged, of achieving its whole potential, of being brought to its goal.

It takes action of the right kind to unlock faith's resources fully, and to carry it on to its true consummation in a miracle.

Christ compelled people to face this principle. He told a lame man to stand up and walk, and a blind man to go and wash his eyes; he told fishermen to cast their nets into the seemingly empty sea; he told bystanders to roll the stone away from Lazarus' tomb; he told Peter to start walking on water; he told the disciples to start handing out a few pieces of bread to a vast crowd; and so on.

In all of those instances, Christ pressed people to act their faith, to start doing the impossible, to do what they could not do before. Faith had to be released by action. And that action had to correspond with the situation into which they were directing their faith. Until they did this, their faith lay fallow. It remained lifeless and ineffective, a promise unfulfilled.

It is hard to imagine a faith situation which does not require some kind of matching action.

That action may be no more than a bold confession, laying claim to the answer as though it had already happened. But something more than words is often called for. Deeds are often required as well, deeds that conform to the thing you are confessing.

Thus James writes:

> *"If a brother or sister is ill clad and lacking daily food, and one of you says to them, 'Go in peace, be warmed and filled', without giving them the things*

> *needed for the body, what does it profit? So faith by itself, if it has no works, is dead" (Ja 1:14-17).*

He means that faith which claims Christ as Saviour will show itself in loving actions not merely loving words. He might also mean that it is vain to tell people to trust God for their food and clothing unless you are willing to do what you can yourself to help them. Your words of faith to them are meaningless unless your actions correspond.

What **your** proper works should be in the faith situation you are facing is something you will need to discover for yourself. Perhaps you will find an example in scripture, or from the experience of another child of God; perhaps a friend will guide you, or the Holy Spirit will speak to you through prayer. But if works are demanded, then faith will remain dead without them. **Faith is completed when it is crowned by action.**

SIGHT - "EIDOS"

> *"For we walk by means of faith, not by means of external appearances" (2 Co 5:7)*

Paul uses a causative preposition (*dia*) to show that the governing factor in his life was not external appearance, but faith. His path was charted, his actions were determined, **not by the dictates of his natural senses, but by the demands of faith.**

The vision faith embraced was a thing more real to him than the sight of his eyes. Faith was the impulse behind his walk, the instrument by which he was guided, the chief agent through which he sought to fulfil his destiny. By means of faith alone he expected to reach his goal. His entire profession was after the manner of faith.

If faith saw things his eye did not see, then he reckoned that faith was in sharper focus, and he chose to live by its truer vision. To him the evidence faith gave was always decisive. Whenever any conflict arose between the claims of faith and those of sight, faith was always declared victorious, and **its** dictates were obeyed.

This is a choice we all must make. Which will dominate: **faith**, or **sight**?

If **sight**, then your soul will remain earth-bound, never able to escape the imprisonment of natural law nor the limitations of this worldly sphere.

But if **faith**, then access will be given you into the holiest, into the glorious presence of God, where the only restriction is the boundary of his almost limitless promise!

Which brings me to the next word:

FULL ASSURANCE - *"PLEROPHORIA"*

> *"For our gospel came to you not in word only, but also in power, and in the Holy Spirit, and in much full assurance" (1 Th 1:5).*

Paul joins two superlatives here: "much" (***polus***) and "full assurance" (***plerophoria***). Those two words convey the sheer extravagance of the victory faith brings when it is linked with the power of the Holy Spirit. Signs, wonders, and miracles become the ordinary experience of such faith!

For that kind of faith there can be no possible defeat; in any situation it remains triumphant!

> *"Since we have a great priest over the house of God, let us draw near with a true heart in full assurance of faith" (He. 10:22).*

Now Paul joins two synonyms, "faith" and "full assurance", for if faith is not **full assurance** then it is nothing.

To have faith is to have complete confidence.

To have faith is to see the full discharge of all that God has promised.

To have faith is to be firmly persuaded that no word of God can fail.

Faith walks boldly into the holiest, expecting a full measure of divine grace, never doubting that God will carry out his promise to the letter.

In this **full assurance** faith recognises no failure, nor accepts any authority except its own under God. It laughs at the pretensions of natural wisdom, at the fickle evidence of the senses, at the false accusations of distorted conscience, at the lies of Satan, and mocks everything that opposes the word of God.

Nothing speaks convincingly to faith except the voice of God. To faith every other voice is suspect. But when God speaks faith rejoices to believe and obey!

This **full assurance** finds its source in two things -

The Priestly Ministry Of Christ

If Christ had not made atonement for our sins, if he were not in heaven interceding for us, if he did not act as our unfailing advocate, then we could never have any hope of approaching God. But now we have this marvellous consolation and restoration given to us:

> *"When Christ had offered for all time a single sacrifice for sins, he sat down at the right hand of God ... For by a single offering he has perfected for all time those who are sanctified ... Therefore brethren, since we have confidence to enter the sanctuary by the blood of Jesus ... and since we have a great high priest over the house of God, let us draw near with a true heart in **full assurance of faith**" (He 10:11-22).*

A True Heart

That is, one that is unfeigned; not pretending sincerity, but truly sincere; not putting on a show of faith, but genuinely believing. It is the heart of a man who has deeply resolved to walk the way of faith, not sight; who deliberately sets his mind on God's word, making it his highest authority, his chief mentor.

A **true** heart is one that is all it claims to be; it is free from deceit.

The Greek adjective is *alethinos,* and it is difficult to express in English. It describes something that is as good as its name. Thus, a "true" army is an army indeed, one fully deserving the title; "true" gold is pure unadulterated metal, every whit as valuable as it appears to be; a "true" man is one who realises to the full the ideal of manhood, one who lacks nothing of the idea, the image, contained in the word "man".

In a Christian, a **true heart** is not merely one that tells the truth, but rather one that is completely **true to the character** it is supposed to represent - that is, the character of a redeemed life. Its Christian likeness is not painted on its surface; it does not merely have a veneer of righteousness. No matter how deeply you cut it, no matter how you test it in the crucible of affliction, no matter what pressure you place it under, no matter how you examine it, the same true character always appears. There is nothing plastic or artificial about it. It is Christian through and through.

Which is only to say that faith and pretense have no part in each other. Faith must be sincere before it can be assured. But this sincerity is not something we can conjure up by ourselves. Its source is in Christ, our High Priest, and in our dependency on the one eternal sacrifice he has made, by which he has perfected for all time those who call upon him in their need.

AMEN - "AMEN"

> *"No matter how many promises God has made, they are `Yes' in Christ. And so through him the `Amen' is spoken by us to the glory of God" (2 Co 1:20, NIV).*

Christ is God's guarantee that all his promises are reliable, and that they will be fulfilled to anyone who believes them. No matter what area of life the promise covers - whether salvation, healing, deliverance, strength, finance, guidance, personal, family - you can trust it completely.

Christ looked at the promises, said "Yes" to them, and was so convinced of their value that he was prepared to die to secure their fulfilment in your life. The death, resurrection, and ascension of Christ place an eternal affirmative seal on all of the wonderful promises of God. They have been made absolutely certain. They are now fully secured.

This emphatic "Yes" by the Saviour means that the promises, no matter how many they are, "shall all certainly be fulfilled; there shall be no vacillation on the part of God; no fickleness; no abandoning of his gracious intention" (Albert Barnes).

But the actual realisation of these guaranteed promises depends on an equally emphatic affirmative response from us. If Christ has pronounced the "**Yes**" we must declare the "**Amen!**"

His word must be matched by **yours**.

If the "**Amen**" does not spring to your lips when you hear his "**Yes**" then the promise will not reach you, its benefit will not be discharged.

Just as the "**Yes**" represents **all** that Christ said and did on our behalf, so the "**Amen**" represents our complete faith response to his promise. It includes both the way we speak and the way we act. The confession of our lips must reveal confidence in the promise; the way we behave must expose our certainty that the promise will be fulfilled for us through Christ; the tenor of our lives must display an eager expectation of the good thing God has spoken. Every fibre of our being must resonate with that joyful "**AMEN!**"

Paul applies the "Yes" to the whole range of promises God has given you in Christ. In actual practice, though, what you need is a "Yes" from Christ to the particular promise that covers your present situation.

Suppose you are sick. In that case you need to secure the "Yes" of the Great Physician to a promise of healing. One of God's many healing promises needs to be quickened in your spirit by Christ, through the Holy Spirit.

But once you hear him say to you, "Yes! that promise is yours! Believe it and be made whole!" then the "Amen!" must leap out of your faith. Boldly you confess that healing is yours. Expectantly you wait for its manifestation. Confidently, and never doubting, you command the sickness to remove itself, speaking with faith's authority. Gladly you praise God, giving him glory through Christ, knowing that the work is already done!

Thus your actions, your words, express the "Amen!" that is in your heart.

In this matter, it is interesting to note that Paul, in the Greek text, did not write simply "Yes" and "Amen". He turned both words into nouns and emphasised them, by adding the article; hence, "**the** Yes", and "**the** Amen". The "Yes" was a particular act of divine commitment the "Amen" was a particular act of human confirmation.

The "Yes" and the "Amen" are the **assured promise** of God and the **faith confession** of man meeting together in Christ, to produce a miracle for the glory of God.

It is my prayer that the Master may use these lessons as an instrument of his "Yes!" to you, and that the response in your heart and on your lips as you close this last page, will be a joyous "**AMEN!**"

BIBLIOGRAPHY

Daily Study Bible, The; William Barclay; The St. Andrew Press, Edinburgh; 1962.

Deliverance From Fear; *Pamphlet*; Leo C. Harris.

Five Keys of Authority; Leo Harris; Crusader Publications; 95 Wattle St. Fullerton.

Greek Myths, The; Vols. 1&2; Penguin Books; UK 1975.

Law of Faith, The; Norman Grubb; Lutterworth Press, London, 1955.

Master Key Of Faith, The; Gordon Cove; Coulton and Co. Printers.

New Testament Word Studies; 1971 reprint by Kregel Publications; Grand Rapids, Michigan.

Notes on the Bible; Albert Barnes (1798-1870).

Power With God Through Fasting and Prayer; Franklin Hall; 1950.

What Luther Says; compiled by E. W. Plass; Concordia Publishing House; Saint Louis, Missouri, 1959.

What You Say Is What You Get; Don Gossett; Whitaker House; Springdale, Pennsylvania, 1976.

Your Faith is Power; Leo Harris; Crusader Publications; 95 Wattle St. Fullerton.

www.ingramcontent.com/pod-product-compliance
Lightning Source LLC
Chambersburg PA
CBHW061312110426
42742CB00012BA/2161